Stressed:

It Changed Everything

Eric Clauss

ISBN: 978-0-9906620-0-6

Edited by Gary M. Clauss, Jr.

Printed in the United States of America.

Contact author at ericclauss99@gmail.com

www.liveonpurpose.training

10 9 8 7 6 5 4 3 2

Disclaimer

The information contained in this book is designed for informative purposes only. I am not a trained counselor and am purely sharing my story. If you identify with any parts of my experience, I encourage you to seek professional counseling.

The material contained in this book is accurate and true to the best of my knowledge and recollection. I've gone through painstaking efforts to make sure that the details are correct. That being said, some of the names and minor details of the events have been changed to protect those involved.

www.liveonpurpose.training

For more information, please email:

ericclauss99@gmail.com

Forward

I've known Eric for several years, and over the years we have become great friends and he has shared many parts of his story with me. After many conversations and finally getting to read Eric's book, it gives me another level of appreciation of Eric's friendship and leadership. There are not many people in this world that could survive what Eric has survived. I thank God for hearing his cry and for carrying him through the storm. Eric by far is an amazing person, friend and mentor to all. I know from being around Eric's family he is a great father and husband who always put his family values first. I personally have mentioned to my wife, Tanya, how Eric has inspired me to become a better father and husband. I believe that things happen for a reason and God puts people in your path. I can truly say that Eric and his inspiring story is a true testimony and has made a difference in my life.

Phillip Sanderson, NREMT-P, BS, MHA

Chief Operating Officer of a large healthcare transport company

Thanks

I would like to thank my wife and children for their love and support as I pursued my passion to help others. They have stood by me every step of the journey and I thank God for them every day. They are my inspiration, encouragement and are the greatest joy in my life.

Special Thanks

A special thanks to my brother Gary who worked incredibly hard and challenged me to create a book that would significantly impact many lives. His commitment and dedication is truly inspiring and I look forward to working on future projects with him.

Dedication

I'd like to dedicate this book to all of the professionals that serve our community and our country every day. Your work is a true gift to everyone, and I feel honored to have met so many of you over the years. Thank you for your service, dedication, and commitment; you have greatly and positively impacted my life.

Chapter

1

I arrived at work at 6:45 a.m. on a beautiful spring morning. The morning air was crisp and cool as I got out of my truck. I glanced over at the two ambulances that were parked in front of the station I was assigned to for the day. I unloaded my truck of all the items I would need for the 24-hour shift: rescue gear, medication kit, spare uniform, sleeping bag, pillow, and some snacks. I entered the station and was met with exhausted eyes and small groans from the off-going team; it had been a rough night. It was always a relief to see the next crew coming in because it meant your shift was almost over. My partner, John, arrived a few minutes later, and we exchanged friendly greetings. John and I, along with the off-going crew, walked to the ambulance to receive a report of important details about the past shift: previous day's calls, equipment used, maintenance issues, supplies that were used, and potential blood and other things that may be lingering in hidden places. After we had finished, last night's crew went back into the station to finish paperwork and reports before checking out and heading home. John and I spent about 30 minutes inspecting the equipment to make sure we were prepared for any emergency that would come our way during the shift.

After all the equipment had been checked, we were finally ready to tackle the long shift that awaited us. We cranked up the ambulance and headed to a local diner to have breakfast. Mike and Ted were the other paramedics that were assigned to our station for the day, and they were directly behind us. On any given shift, there were ten EMS teams assigned to different units throughout the county. Crews would often meet at small restaurants to have meals, and it was a great way to catch-up on what we did on our days off, or talk about family stuff. Paramedics and firefighters, along with most other para-military professionals, develop and extremely close bond with their team-members; we were a dysfunctional family, of sorts. We would play practical jokes on one another as often as we could, knowing deep down that we may be trusting each other with our lives in a moment's notice.

After breakfast, we all headed back to the station to start on our tasks and assignments for the day. John and Mike were in the office filling out paperwork, and Ted and I were in the ambulance bay, cleaning. We were engaged in light conversation; then Ted paused and looked at me with a very serious face. He said, "Eric, I have to tell you something." He paused as if he wasn't sure how to go on, but the door was open, and there was no turning back. He went on, "You are going to think I'm crazy when I tell you this, Eric." Another pause. I looked at him and wondered what was about to come out of his mouth that was so serious. He continued, "I have been having some problems with thoughts that come into my head, and I can't control them. They are of my family being killed... and I am the one killing them. Eric, I don't want to kill my wife and kids, but these thoughts won't leave my mind no matter what I do. They are just there, always, and it's freaking me out!"

I couldn't believe what I was hearing, and I wanted to speak, but nothing came out. I searched my heart for the right words to say, and the silence was deafening. My mind was racing in all directions and my heart was pounding out of my chest. "Ted, it's got to be the stress of the job that's causing this," I said. We talked for a few more moments about it, and then we went on as if it had never happened.

I didn't tell Ted that there was one thing ironic about his experience; I had been having thoughts of my family dying for years and never told anyone. Ted and I were good friends, and we had worked together for eleven years. I often wanted to talk with him again in more detail about his thoughts, my thoughts, but I never did. I didn't want to admit to myself that this was not normal, and if I just continued to ignore the thoughts, they would go away. The thoughts didn't go away though, and the perfect storm was stirring inside me; a storm that would nearly cost me my life.

Chapter

2

I grew up in the inner city of Baltimore, Maryland, and lived there for the first ten years of my life. It was the 1970's, and as I remember, it was a great place to live. Several relatives, including my grandparents, lived within walking distance to our home. My brother Gary and I would often play with our cousins: riding bicycles, skateboarding, or just running around playing childhood games. During the school year, we would walk about twenty minutes to school every day, and that was so much fun for us. Several of the neighborhood kids, my cousins, my brother and I would walk together to and from school every day, laughing and just being kids. Occasionally on the way home we would stop at the corner store and get a 25-cent cola or some candy. Across from the corner store was the local

Stressed: It Changed Everything

Baltimore City Fire Station that was in our neighborhood. I would often stare and daydream of driving the fire truck or ambulance, or riding on the back-step of the fire truck as it sped through the streets, lights flashing and sirens blaring, on their way to whatever new adventure was awaiting them.

My grandparents lived across the street from us, and our family was extremely close. My grandmother would often watch my brother and me, along with our other cousins, when our parents worked. My grandfather was a deputy sheriff for the City of Baltimore and was an avid baseball player in his younger days. They both worked for the election board, and at that time you had to go to a government building to vote. Schools were closed on Election Day, so we had the whole day free to run and play. In our neighborhood, the voting was held at the local Baltimore City Fire Department, so my grandmother would be at the firehouse all day supervising the voting process, and it provided a great opportunity for me to visit and watch the activities in the firehouse.

The fire station was on the corner of a busy four-lane street, in a section of row homes that were common in our neighborhood. The inside of the fire station was fairly small and resembled a large garage, with one big difference... in the middle was a larger-than-life fire truck that sparkled. The truck was red and white, and was so clean that it seemed to glow. The truck's wheels were almost as big as me, with polished rims. A cabin with a single red-dome bubble light on top that would spin as they were responding to emergencies, with the piercing shriek of the siren that warned everyone that they were coming. The back of the truck had a large step where the firefighters would stand as they responded to emergencies, and above the step you could see the large hose fanned out that they used to fight fires. That back step seemed to call to me and invite me to sit upon it, as I dreamed of what it was like to ride to emergencies while standing tall and proud. At the back of the station bay was a small kitchenette and a giant hose tower. The walls of the bay were lined with rows of turnout gear that were stained with ash and soot from the many fires that were fought. The brass pole that was used to get from the second-story bedroom area was at the back of the station, and seemed to sparkle like a golden pole to heaven. When you walked into the fire station, you were greeted with the smell that is unique to firehouses everywhere; a pungent mixture of rubber, smoke, truck exhaust, diesel fuel, and other unknown fumes smacked you in the face as you walked in the door. To this day I still remember the smell of that station, and anytime I walk in a fire house, it takes me back to memory lane. This was as close to a superhero's secret hideaway I could imagine; the alarm rings, the superheroes slide down the pole and get into their gear, then they get into the truck that would take them to save lives and fight fires.

My dreams of becoming a firefighter became even more vivid one afternoon while visiting the fire station. One of the firefighters asked me if I wanted to sit in the passenger seat of the engine, and I gladly accepted. I was sitting there, with a huge smile on my face, imagining what it would be like to actually ride to an emergency. Suddenly, the alarm sounded! I will never forget the sound of that alarm going off, and watching before my eyes the firefighters scrambling to get into their gear and find their places on the truck. The captain lifted me out of the truck and placed me beside my grandmother, and together we watched the truck pull out of the garage with lights flashing and siren blaring. My heart was racing, and my eyes were huge as I took it all in, while squeezing my grandmother's hand.

Those memories are still quite vivid in my mind, and serve as a constant reminder of why I do what I do. When I reflect back, it's almost as if it chose me, instead of me choosing it as a career.

Chapter

3

When I was eleven we moved from Baltimore City to the suburbs, which was very exciting. I was still young, so the adjustment to a different lifestyle came quite naturally. I made new friends in our neighborhood and at school, and life was pretty good. I progressed through junior high school as any pre-teen boy does, discovering my strengths and weaknesses, likes and dislikes. I had several good friends, hated homework, and loved playing baseball.

When I started high school, I decided to try out for the baseball team. I was excited and nervous initially, but my love for the sport took over, and I made the team. Cooler temperatures often linger through the spring in Maryland, and because of that, practice would be tough. During one practice, the coach made us run laps around the field. I paced myself and ended up in the back of the pack with a guy named Tommy. We began to talk, and quickly realized that we lived in the same neighborhood. Tommy and I connected, and we became best friends almost immediately. Tommy was a humorous young man, very quick-witted, and could make you laugh until it hurt. He owned a lawn-care business, played baseball, was an incredible golfer, and went to school, all without missing a beat. He was, and still is, one of the hardest working people I've ever known, and yet he was always full of energy. Tommy and I were very close, and we were together all the time. His family also loved me, and they became like a second family. His mom was very sweet, and an amazing cook, and would invite me to dinner all the time. I have countless memories of eating and laughing at their dinner table, sharing stories with his parents and his younger brother and sister.

One of the first times I was at his house, we were sitting and talking, and suddenly there was a loud horn blaring outside. It was so loud that it startled me and made me jump. Tommy laughed, and we went on talking. A moment later I heard a fire truck race by with its siren blaring. I asked Tommy about it, and he told me that it was the horn for the volunteer fire station, and it would blow to alert the firefighters in the area that there was an emergency. My curiosity was officially piqued! A fire station of volunteers!

One afternoon at baseball practice, Tommy told me that he was going to join the volunteer fire department. He was going to train to become a firefighter and emergency medical technician (EMT). I was startled. We had just turned 16; how was this possible? I will never forget that day and the feelings and emotions that buzzed through my mind. I instantly remembered the dream I had as a small boy of becoming a firefighter. When we were younger, my brother and I would often pretend to be firefighters and paramedics, thanks to the popular television show *Emergency*. I couldn't believe that at the age of 16 you could volunteer as a firefighter, if your parents consented. It was all I could think about for weeks. Could it be, that my childhood dream would become a reality while I was still in high school? I sat down with my mom, and after I had explained all the details, she was completely supportive.

I put in my application at the fire department in the summer of 1985, and I was so excited that I could barely contain myself. There was an interview by a few officers of the department, and then all the members would vote on whether to allow the applicant to become a probationary member. The probationary period lasted several months, and all attendance, training, and conduct were monitored. Once the probationary period ended, the entire department would vote again and decide on whether to allow you to become an official member. My application was accepted, and I became a probationary member. The first few weeks I would hang out at the station and ask many questions. Since I hadn't officially taken any classes nor had any training, I wasn't allowed to respond to any emergencies, so I'd look over every piece of equipment, visualizing what it was like to use it on a fire or rescue.

The fire station was huge, with five bays, living and sleep quarters, training classrooms, gym area, and a training tower in the back. It was equipped with two ambulances, two engines, a brush-fire jeep, a mini pumper, and a rescue squad. There were over fifty active volunteers, and eight career-firefighters at the station as well. My favorite piece of equipment was the rescue squad. Squad 1 was a beast of a rescue truck that held seven members: two in the cab and five in the back. The squad was covered with doors that housed any piece of equipment needed for a rescue. The inside compartment where the firefighters would sit was also filled with anything that couldn't fit in the compartments covering the outside of the truck. The squad was equipped with enough lights to make any accident scene light up as if it were happening in the middle of a professional sports stadium. The squad was the envy of every department in the county, and was often called upon to go to incidents that weren't even in our jurisdiction because of its capabilities. In my opinion, it should've been called Mega Squad 1!

A few weeks after I became a member I started my first class, along with a few other team members from the station. This first class was the basic firefighting course and lasted eighty hours. All the classes were taught by the University of Maryland Fire and Rescue Institute instructors. The class was taught at another station in the county, and everyone from our station that was enrolled would meet and ride together in one of the station's utility vehicles. We would put all of our brand new turnout gear in the back and head down the road anticipating what new adventure awaited us in class that night. I went to high school during the day, and two nights a week attended firefighting school. The first few classes dealt with the science of fire, how it thinks and acts. We then moved on to the practice of how to actually put out a fire. That class was an experience I will truly cherish, not only because it was fun and exciting, but it was also my first real experience with discipline and how to handle situations that were unpredictable and dangerous. Teamwork was engrained in us from the very beginning because it could make the difference between life and death. Our class was strong, and we developed a tight bond unlike anything I had ever experienced.

Midway through the class we had to take a mid-term exam, and not only did this test determine whether you could finish the class or not, it was also the point where passing meant you could begin riding on the emergency response vehicles. Granted, you were only allowed to observe until you finished the training, it was still an exciting opportunity to see what you were learning actually practiced in real life. There was a written and practical part to the exam, and we were all nervous, because we wanted to feel that adrenaline rush of helping at an emergency scene, no matter how small the role.

Part of the mid-term was putting on your full turnout gear in under a minute: fire-resistant pants, boots, hood, jacket, helmet, and gloves. We all practiced daily, because each additional piece of gear you put on it got more bulky and cumbersome to do anything else, and this added extra weight to your body. We all passed and were able to move forward.

One aspect of our training that was highly anticipated by the class was the day we got to go through the training maze. All the veteran firefighters and instructors would talk about this day and tell stories that caused fear and excitement at the same time. It was almost seen as a rite of passage among firefighters.

These mazes contained obstacles that were often encountered in real situations; however, the inside of the mazes were painted black and were often filled with smoke. Because of this, the trainees had to wear full turnout gear, in addition to a large air tank strapped to their back, connected to a mask covering their face. These mazes were often in trailers so they could be moved and used in many locations, and some had multiple levels. The fear of the unknown made you weak in the knees, as you stood in line waiting for your turn. The trainees that went in before you came out the other side, so you didn't know what to expect or how long it took to get through. As you entered, you had to immediately get on your hands and knees because many of the passages were too small to stand. As you progressed on, there were spots that were so narrow that you couldn't fit through while wearing all of your equipment, so you had to remove your air tank and feed it through the tight passages before you could fit through yourself. These mazes were definitely no place for those who suffered from claustrophobia. It was dark and you felt like you were alone in this funhouse of horrors, hearing every breath as it escaped from your mask, feeling your way inch by inch for any hazards that were waiting. There were always instructors watching over you to help if you encountered problems or started to panic. I never panicked, but there were times when I wasn't sure if I'd make it through. That training day seemed to go on forever, but it was an exhilarating experience.

Even though that initial training class lasted only eighty-hours, it set a foundation that would be built upon with everything else you did, and I'm still building upon that foundation today. At the end of that class, I felt a great sense of accomplishment, and that increased my confidence level.

Chapter

4

After we had completed that initial firefighting training course, we were allowed to participate in firefighting and rescue activities. New team members were considered rookies, and were required to wear a big, red "R" on their helmets so that the other experienced firefighters would know to keep an eye on them. You didn't have to wear the "R" for very long, and we'd do whatever we could to get those R's off of our helmets. Looking back on that time now, maybe I would've kept and respected the need for that "R" a little longer.

I can remember the first time I rode Engine 11 to an emergency. Tommy and I were hanging out at his house, and the siren blared to alert everyone that there was an emergency call. We immediately ran to the firehouse and quickly got into our gear and hopped on the back-step of the engine, hitting the buzzer to let the driver know we were secured and ready to go. We took off, lights flashing and sirens blaring. I'm sure I had a huge smile plastered on my face; I was 16 and this wasn't a dream anymore, it was real. The air-horn blasted a few times, warning the cars at the intersection that we were approaching, and they needed to stop or get out of the way. I had such a feeling of elation on that first call, and that feeling never dwindled, but only got more intense with every response I made at the fire station.

Shortly after my basic firefighting training, I responded to a call on a busy highway that ran through our district. This highway was always busy, and with the speed that cars were traveling, the accidents are always serious. This accident included two vehicles with several patients trapped in each car. Our chief asked me to assist with extricating one of the patients trapped in one of the cars. One of the EMT's crawled into the vehicle to provide neck stabilization and begin the initial assessment of the patient while we used hydraulic power tools to gain access. This power tool was able to slice through metal as if it was butter, and was amazing to see in action. After all the cuts had been made, we removed the door and part of the roof, then placed them to the side. I picked up the backboard

Eric Clauss

and held it while the EMT's removed the patient and continued providing treatment. I could only watch and support the patient on the backboard as the medical team secured him and determined that he needed extensive treatment.

Our station was relatively close to the University of Maryland's Shock Trauma Center, and we would often drive critical patients via ambulance, rather than calling for Maryland State Police Medevac helicopter. We loaded the patient into the ambulance, and I was in the back helping the medic get situated; the door closed, and we were off to Shock Trauma. Everyone was so engrossed in helping the patient, I'm not sure they realized I was even there, but I could hold things and hand them any equipment they needed, and extra hands are always appreciated. I felt overwhelmed and helpless as we sped toward Shock Trauma, just watching the medics perform their medical procedures on the patient while they talked on the radio to the staff of the hospital alerting them that they were coming.

Dropping off a patient at a trauma center is a surreal experience. You are met at the door by a large team of doctors, nurses, and technicians that sweep the patient away, and each begins their assessment and treatment with precision and focus that is truly awe-inspiring, especially for someone who has no

19

medical training. The medics passed off the patient to the trauma staff, and gave a report in what seemed to be a foreign language, as I just stood there like a wallflower with wide eyes absorbing it all. We piled into the back of the ambulance and headed back to the station while I replayed the situation over and over in my head. I came to the realization that I could serve the team better if I had more training, and I decided to enroll in the EMT training class.

Chapter

5

The EMT Class was held at a local community college, and once again was taught by a University of Maryland Fire and Rescue Institute Instructor. Just like the basic firefighting class, the EMT class included members from across the county, and about a third of this class were students from our station. My brother Gary was in this class with me, and we became very close. Our class was taught by a firefighter/paramedic lieutenant from our station, who was also a full-time instructor for the University of Maryland, Greg was truly one of the smartest people I have ever known. This class was 120 hours, and we met twice a week for an entire semester. The class was intense, and the material was challenging, with each week building upon the previous lesson. Greg kept the class fun, while stressing how important all of the information was to retain. This class provided a great foundation for emergency care.

While progressing through the class, I was still active as a firefighter in the department, and was beginning to see things through new eyes. At first it was intimidating being on a call with your instructor, but he had a way of making you feel at ease and would point things out and show you hands-on what and how things worked in real life situations. He not only was an amazing instructor in the class, but was great to work with on the scene of an actual emergency. When I look back now, I cherish those moments, and am grateful that I had the opportunity to not only learn from the best, but to see how they worked in the field.

We had passed the mid-term point in the class, and Gary and I were home studying one evening. We heard on our pagers that there was an emergency medical services (EMS) call right down the street from our house, a pedestrian hit by a car! Gary and I looked at each other and bolted for the door. As we hopped into my 1972 bug and raced to the scene, we heard the voice of our instructor on the pager; Greg was at the station and was on the ambulance responding to the call. My heart raced; an opportunity to be first on the scene of an actual emergency and our instructor is on the way to see how good we are and how much we've learned! We had no equipment with us, and nothing that really even identified us as health-care providers. We arrived on the scene, and sure enough, there was a guy laying on the side of the road; Gary grabbed his head to hold neck stabilization in case there was a neck injury, and I began doing a head-to-toe survey and patient assessment. We didn't say anything to the guy, because we were both so nervous, and we were going over in our minds exactly what we needed to do and what steps to take. Because the ambulance hadn't arrived yet, I can only imagine what this guy was thinking, "Who are these kids? Why are they holding me down? And why in the world are they rubbing all over me?" A few minutes later the ambulance arrived, and Greg walks over to us and asks what we have. He then bent down and asked the patient this simple question, "Hey buddy, what happened?" The guy responds, "I've been drinking a little, and was trying to walk home. This car pulled up and stopped, a guy got out and punched me, then he drove away." The guy hadn't been hit by a car at all; he was hit by a guy in a car! Greg smiled and patted us on the back, seeing that we had tried so hard to do things right. The guy declined treatment, and didn't need to be transported to the hospital. I learned a valuable lesson that evening that can't be taught in class; talk to your patients, they can provide tons of details. While a very humbling experience, Greg used it as a teaching moment. He saw that we had learned a lesson that isn't in any textbook. Gary and I still laugh at that story to this day.

Many do not fully appreciate the training, roles, and responsibilities of EMT's. They are a vital part of communities today, especially those that volunteer. They are often the first on the scene of an emergency, and the training is thought to be so important that many cities will cross-train firefighters as EMT's so there will always be someone with medical training on the scene. EMT's are trained to recognize and begin treatment on a whole spectrum of medical emergencies: from a sprained ankle to a multi-level trauma patient, from a mild cough to a heart attack. They not only have to deal with the patient, but also the friends and family members who are seeing their loved one in distress. On top of this, they often have to handle bystanders who are engrossed in watching this drama unfold as if it were a scene from a live-action, medical thriller on television. They have to be scene commanders, and coordinate rescue, fire, and med-evac services. It is not just a job that you do from 9 to 5; it is what you become and who you are.

As our class progressed and became more intense, with more information to memorize on top of retaining everything we learned in the previous weeks, the class became very close, and we developed a strong bond. We had highs and lows, and with the mid-term behind us and the final approaching, we all felt lots of stress, because we realized that not only were these scenarios from class just theories in a book, they were going to be played out daily in our lives. In EMS, your effectiveness to deliver patient care increases when you know your partner like you know the back of your hand. You must have mutual trust and respect and confidence in your partner, knowing each other's strengths and weaknesses, and be able to play off of them, and in turn they can do the same for you. My strength and passion at the time was firefighting, and I made this no secret to anyone, while Gary seemed to pick up things in the class naturally. Gary was book smart, and he seemed to be able to process all this material with no problem, and it became obvious that his strength was going to be EMS. Because of this, it seemed only fitting that I'd choose my brother as my partner. The material was overwhelming at times, but the class often had study sessions to help each other. I stayed focused on the goal knowing that if I passed the class I'd be a Firefighter/EMT who could better serve the community and department. I got through the class, and I'm still thankful for that instructor who taught me the basics and laid the foundation for my career in the medical field.

Stressed: It Changed Everything

Chapter

6

Excitement was in the air at the department when word began to spread about an upcoming training fire. Occasionally, someone from the community would donate a house to the fire department for training purposes. These homes were often old and in poor condition, but provided a great opportunity for firefighters to gain experience with real fire in a semi-controlled situation. Senior firefighters and instructors always supervised these training fires; however, fire is living and breathing and does not always perform in a predictable way.

It was a crisp, fall morning, and we all arrived at the location of the house-burning. After the house was thoroughly inspected, and a detailed briefing was given to all participants, the fun began. The instructors would gather wood and straw and light it on fire in a corner of a room in the house; then the firefighters would enter the house, search for the fire location and extinguish it. These exercises would continue as long as the structure of the house was strong and safe. The department usually divided the participants into teams of five, and the teams usually contained both well-seasoned and inexperienced firefighters. The teams were rotating through the exercises; some were excited, some were nervous. Black smoke started to fill the sky, and by-standers started to gather to watch our training.

Finally, the time came for my team to enter the house. We grabbed the hose, and started to enter the structure as a group, on our knees, being led by the nozzle-man. I was fourth from the nozzle, and directly behind me was the senior firefighter of our group, Bill. We crawled through the hot, smoke-filled house until we located the room that was on fire. Bill had many years of firefighting experience, was a great leader and teacher, and was someone you could trust in any situation, so I felt lucky to be on his team. He was able to keep his cool, no matter how hot the situation, and seemed to be able to read the mind of the fire; he was truly a well-seasoned firefighter. The fire we were pursuing was in a bedroom at the end of a narrow hall. The room was so small that only three firefighters could fit in the area with the hose. The first three team-members entered the room to extinguish the fire while Bill and I stayed in the hall controlling the hose-line, and standing by for support if needed. The firefighters in the room were not able to see us, and we were not able to see them. The hall was lightly filled with smoke, and there was sunlight coming through a window in an adjacent room. The sounds of water spraying and the fire popping echoed over the sound of our breath escaping from the breathing apparatus we were wearing.

A moment later, I heard the sound of what seemed to be a rushing train and a tornado mixed together, and it was getting louder. Bill screamed my name from behind, I turned around to see him, and was overtaken with fear. A giant fireball from floor to ceiling was heading toward us. The sound getting louder and deeper, the heat growing more intense, the orange glow penetrating the darkness. In that instant, I was paralyzed by fear; I thought I was going to be burned alive and probably die. Suddenly, I felt the weight of Bill as he jumped on top of me and pushed me to the floor, covering me as much as possible from this impending doom that was about to overtake both of us. The flames of that fireball engulfed us, and they passed over us. The sound was deafening, the heat more intense than anything I've ever imagined. As quickly as it began, the flash was over. While that moment seemed like an eternity, in reality it was only a few seconds. Bill crawled off of me, and I was disoriented, confused, and was wondering how badly I was burned. Bill was yelling through his mask, "Eric, are you okay?" I wanted to answer, but couldn't respond. We were both covered in debris that was still burning, and we were doing our best to brush it off and put it out.

The rescue team that was on stand-by rushed in and grabbed Bill and me and drug us down the hall and out of the house as if we were rag-dolls. The rescue operation happened so quickly and was so swift that I thought I had to be badly burned. Once outside the house, the stress and panic of the situation overtook me, and I became overwhelmed with emotion and felt helpless. My fellow firefighters wrestled to get me out of my breathing apparatus, and removed my turnout gear with incredible speed. All I could do was stand there and watch, shocked by the events that took place over the past three minutes. Gary happened to be the EMT on stand-by, and fortunately neither Bill nor I received any burns or serious injuries that day. When I think back to that situation, I picture Bill as a true super-hero. He risked his life to jump on and protect me without even thinking. In a matter of seconds, we were in a life-threatening situation, and his first thought was to protect his team-members. The rescue team was also selfless, in that they ran into a dangerous situation, risking their own lives to save others. I was beginning to understand how life-altering and dangerous this career would be.

I feel so fortunate to have met so many great role-models while volunteering at that fire department. They guided me not only on the path of my career, but they helped me through those tough, teenage years. As the months went by, I was starting to realize that a career in emergency services was for me, and deep down I knew this was my calling, and this is what I was meant to do.

For 24 months I was a member of that department, and I was at the station on-call nearly every evening. The firehouse had a bunk-room with several beds, and I stayed there on many weeknights and weekends. Reflecting back, I'm glad I did not take that time for granted, because I now rely on the lessons learned while there: team-work, respecting authority, having a strong work ethic, trust, and persistence. These things hold a very special place in my life today, and I truly believe it was because of that volunteer experience.

Stressed: It Changed Everything

Chapter

7

When I was 18, I left Maryland and moved to Tennessee. My initial plan was to get a job as a firefighter and build a career in that field. I had training and experience, so I didn't think this would be a problem. After living in Tennessee for a short period of time, I began to realize that my plan to become a firefighter was not likely in the short-term; I discovered that there are very few positions available. Finding work in the emergency services field was my passion, so I began to search other avenues. I was fortunate enough to have met some great EMS workers in the small town where I lived, and they helped me get a position as an EMT in a medium-sized town just south of Nashville. This was a great opportunity for me to continue towards my goal of working in the emergency

Stressed: It Changed Everything

services field, and that ambulance service was a great place to work. I'm very thankful to those people who helped me get my foot in the door, and I'm still in touch with several of them today.

After several months of working there, and surrounding myself with great and encouraging people, I decided to take the next-step and apply to an EMT-Paramedic (EMT-P) program. This was a huge decision for me, and very scary, to say the least. Firefighting and rescue operations were my passion, and while I did okay in the EMT class, I was still intimidated by the medical field. Hopefully, paramedic school was the right step, and what could it hurt to try, I'd just take it one step at a time.

In Maryland at the time, there were very few paramedics, and they were thought to be the best of the best. In most areas in Maryland, you were always only minutes away from a hospital, so staying on the scene to perform extensive medical procedures was often seen as unnecessary. You could call for a Maryland State Police Med-Evac and in minutes a helicopter would be on the scene, with personnel who had advanced medical training, and they would take over treatment and fly the patient to whatever specialty hospital the patient needed. The 911-operators would often call and alert the Med-

Evac service if they thought the call warranted the need, and you'd arrive on the scene and would hear the helicopter overhead. It truly was a great program and was ground-breaking at the time.

However in Tennessee, with many rural areas, it is necessary to provide extensive treatment in the field. Paramedics are widely used, and the skills they possess are not only needed, they are greatly respected. Paramedics act as the eyes, ears, and hands of the physicians in the field, and they have the training and skills to communicate their findings to emergency rooms, and carry out many procedures that can sustain and save lives. It was overwhelming to see first-hand the patient-care they provided, and the skills they used, and I had a chance to work with them daily and see what a difference they made in people's lives.

I applied to and was accepted into the University of Alabama at Huntsville's EMT-Paramedic Program. The application process was very difficult, but nothing intimidated me more than the interview with the Medical Director of the program. The interview lasted about twenty minutes, and just when I thought we were through, he asked a very poignant question. He asked, "How would you react if your treatment caused someone to die? How would you handle that?" I had

Stressed: It Changed Everything

honestly never thought about that before that day, and it forced me to realize how big the responsibility is in becoming a paramedic. After thinking for a moment, I answered, "You have to learn from every situation and improve on every mistake made, so you don't repeat them." I'm not sure if this was the answer he was looking for, and I'm not even sure there is one right answer to that question. I think his goal was to get the students applying to the program to grasp the magnitude of the responsibility that was going to be placed on them. If that was his goal, it worked on me!

I drove to Huntsville, Alabama on the first night of class, and was so nervous. My palms were sweaty, and I could barely concentrate as I made the hour long commute to the campus. I was beginning to question my decision to enroll in the program because I knew that many of the students would fail. In fact, I heard that usually half of the students usually failed or dropped out of the program before it was over; which half of the class would I be part of? Studying had never been one of my strengths, and I knew this was going to be challenging. I tried not to dwell on the big picture, but thought I'd concentrate on taking one step at a time, and tackle each issue as it approached. The class was held in a large lecture hall with theater seating, and when I arrived several people had already taken their seats and were waiting for the instructor. As I looked around the room, most of the other students had worried expressions on their faces, as I'm sure I did as well. I chose a seat, unloaded my backpack, and was ready for the first step.

The instructor entered, and a hush fell over the room. He was a big man and had a very intimidating, stern look on his face. He finally spoke, and with a harsh voice, he said, "My name is Steve, and I'll be your instructor for this portion of the program. Tell me why you are here." A few students were brave enough to speak up, but there was no way I was opening my mouth. After listening to a few of the responses, while pacing the front of the lecture hall, he stopped in front of the podium and picked up a large textbook, one of the manuals we would be studying for this course. He held the book out, with the cover facing the class, and stood there silently. The class just stared, with wide eyes. He threw the book across the room and it crashed in the corner. He bellowed, "This is what this book will mean to you if you manage to graduate from this program!" At this point, only a few minutes into the class, and I was really wondering what I was doing here. He then spoke again, "Look at the person on your left, now look at the person on your right, at least one of you will not be here on graduation day." I was ready to crawl out the door at this point, and hope that no one would notice me. Steve did a great job of intimidating the entire class that first day, using boot-camp tactics to scare the weak away, and it almost worked on me, but I wasn't giving up so quickly. As the class progressed, we got to know and love Steve, and while he had a gruff exterior at times, he was really an amazing man with a giant heart, and possessed a great deal of knowledge.

I had to push myself daily to get through that program. It was fifteen months of studying, and memorizing, and clinical rotations, and written exams, and practical exams. Five semesters with each growing more challenging than the previous, and each new term there were fewer students enrolled. I studied my paramedic textbooks so much that not only could I quote some of the information verbatim, I could usually tell you the page number and where on the page the information was located. Every week, our instructors would put us through scenarios to test our knowledge in stressful situations, these were referred to as mock-codes; nothing causes more stress in a paramedic student's life than getting in front of the class to perform what you have learned on a mannequin. The instructors were tough on us, and at times it seemed they didn't like us at all. There were countless quizzes, and mock-codes, and running through scenarios where it seemed they were intentionally trying to set us up for failure. Seeing the big picture now, they were just preparing us for the real world, where you never know what was going to be thrown at you, because in the field there isn't time to check a textbook or ask an instructor what you should do.

As part of the program, we were required to do clinical rotations through numerous departments in the hospital, as well as ride-along's with the local EMS service in the area. As the day approached for my first paramedic ride-along, I was extremely anxious, even though I had been working in the field for quite some time. I reported for my first shift, and we were not very busy. I sat, trying to study my textbooks, but not really able to concentrate because I was eager for that first 911 call to come in. Hours seemed to pass, and while the regular team I was assigned to seem to be enjoying the little break, I wanted to get on with it, and get my first call as an EMT-P student over with.

The call came in the middle of the afternoon, and we were to respond to a shooting. Up to this point in my career I had worked a few shootings, but now I was to see things as a paramedic, and it made me nervous. I climbed into the back of the unit, and we responded. As we got closer, I started to get more anxious, trying to anticipate what to expect. One great lesson I've learned over the years is that it's best to prepare your mind for the worst case scenario while responding to an emergency, because you truly never know what you will find.

Stressed: It Changed Everything

Once we arrived, there were several bystanders that were obviously shaken by what had happened, and there was a body lying on the ground in the near distance. We walked closer, and I could see there was a large amount of blood pooled around the body and obvious disfigurement of the head. This patient was obviously killed by a single gun-shot wound to the head. It's never easy to see a person who has died just minutes ago, but that is part of this life I've chosen, right? You do your very best to help those you can, and try to quickly get through those you can't, and move on. As we gathered information from the family, we discovered that they were having a picnic and the man pulled out a .44-magnum handgun, placed it to his head, and pulled the trigger... right in front of the family. I often wonder what family members and bystanders have to live with, and the images they are haunted by, when someone they love takes their own life right in front of them. Unfortunately, this was the first of many similar situations I was a part of during my many years in EMS.

As the class progressed, Steve became a mentor and friend to me. I no longer had him as an instructor, but I would often stop by his office to say hello, and he always had words of encouragement for me and told me to keep pressing on. One evening before class I noticed a brochure posted for an advanced cardiac course. This course was going to be taught by several of the instructors from our program, and I knew that I would eventually have to get this certification, but my confidence level wasn't that high, because I was not finished with paramedic training yet. I asked Steve if he would allow me to sit in the class as an observer, just to see what was in store for us in the future. Steve seemed intrigued by my interest, and not only did he encourage me to sit in the class, he told me I should enroll as a student because he thought I would do well. I thought about it, and I enrolled in the course.

The day came for the class, and I arrived early. My nerves had gotten the best of me, which wasn't unusual for me at this point. I had gotten used to the butterflies, and they even seemed to be old friends to me. I walked into the lecture hall, and it was nearly filled with close to one hundred participants. To my surprise, the participants were physicians, nurses, and seasoned paramedics, and this certainly didn't help my comfort level. I felt like a fish out of water, and was completely out of my element, but here I was, and I wasn't turning back. I scanned the class and found a seat in the back of the room, and tried to get settled without drawing attention to myself.

The instructors walked into the amphitheater, and rather than feel nervous by the class starting, I felt comforted by the familiar faces of my instructors who were leading the class. They made their introductions and made everyone feel at ease by telling a few jokes and letting us know what was going to be covered. The instruction portion of the class was first, and they seemed to pour over tons of information, some of which was familiar to me from the paramedic program, but some of it was new knowledge, and I was doing my best to keep up and process everything. The class progressed, and I knew that the much dreaded mock-code scenarios were approaching, but I thought I could learn from watching how physicians and nurses and experienced paramedics handled the situations I was beginning to feel accustomed to in class. The instructors demonstrated the first scenario to show us what was expected, and how to handle a mock-code situation properly. They stressed that it wasn't rehearsed, and you never knew what was going to be thrown at you, and I had learned that lesson all too well in the paramedic program. While I had seen, and even participated in many mock-code scenarios, the one they played out in front of us was the most challenging and difficult I could have ever imagined. The instructor that acted as the participant in the scenario rattled off procedures and medications in a wonderful way that awed everyone: he truly was brilliant, and I gained even more respect for my instructors... not only did they know the information and how to teach it, they could actually handle themselves in stressful situations. At the same time, I was getting anxious because there was no way I could handle the scenario they were playing out. I looked around the room, and many of the other attendees had the same look of horror on their faces as I'm sure I did. They finally ended after what seemed to be an eternity, and turned to the class and said, "This is what you have to look forward to if you want to pass this class." You could hear a pin drop in the class, and these were all professionals who worked in the medical field, so what chance did I have as a beginner? The instructors started to laugh and said, "We are just kidding. You can breathe now." You could hear a collective sigh from the room, and the tension escaped a little, but everyone was still a bit nervous.

One of the instructors said, "What we'd like to do is show you what you can really expect in your mock-code scenario, and we want someone to help us out. Are there any volunteers?" Not a single hand went up in the room, and everyone seemed to sink into their seats all at once. "Well, since no one is volunteering, we'll just pick someone, and I have an individual in mind already," He added. "The person we have in mind has no idea we are going to call on him, and he is not even a paramedic yet. He's still in our paramedic training program," he continued. I quickly scanned the room to search for any familiar faces, as my heart began to jump out of my chest. I certainly wasn't who he was talking about, and if he calls on me, I'll likely be the patient in the mock-code instead of the student! I then heard, "Would you please give a hand for Eric Clauss as he comes up to demonstrate what we are looking for." Oh my goodness, no thank you, certainly not! Everyone clapped as their eyes scanned the room for someone to stand, but I was not about to walk down to the front of the class. The instructor looked at me and encouragingly said, "Come on Eric, come on down." There was no hiding now; he had found me and pointed me out, and now everyone was looking at me. My knees were shaking as I stood, and I felt like I needed to throw-up as I began to make the journey to the front of the lecture hall. As I approached the front, one of the instructors put his arm around me and whispered in my ear, "Eric, you perform mock-codes in my class all the time, and you are excellent. Be confident, and lean on your knowledge, I know you can do it. You can help everyone in this room, and show them how it's done." Those few words of encouragement gave me the boost of confidence I needed, and a sense of calm came over me. I scanned the class, and saw what seemed to be thousands of eyes staring at me as I took a breath and got myself ready. I turned to face the instructor, and he began. The scenario he gave me was of a critical patient that needed rapid assessment and treatment. I approached each step with proficiency and continued through the few curves he threw my way. As quickly as it began, it was over. The instructor turned to the class and said, "This is the way it needs to be done. That is exactly what we expect from every one of you." The class clapped for me as I turned and asked the instructors with a smile, "Will that count as my mock-code for the class?" They laughed and responded, "Absolutely."

The dedication and hard work was paying off, and the instructors saw my potential, and it was encouraging. I continued to press forward with fervor and determination to get through that class and do the best I could.

The program started with nineteen students, and only six of us graduated. After going through that program with those other five people, and seeing the training we had together, I would trust my life in their hands any day. While it may have seemed at times that we were being discouraged while in the class, the instructors were really encouraging us to be better and to press on to be the best that we could be. I have a great deal of respect for each of those instructors, and do my best to honor them with the work I do every day.

Stressed: It Changed Everything

Chapter

8

While in paramedic school, a co-worker thought I'd get along well with his sister-in-law, so he arranged for us to meet for an informal dinner. I arrived at his house to meet them, said hi to him and his wife, and sitting with them was a beautiful girl. He introduced me to Clarissa, and I knew immediately that I could fall in love with her.

Clarissa was also in college at the time, studying to become a radiology technician at a local community college. She came from a strong family with very traditional southern roots. I got along well with her parents and her three sisters.

Clarissa and I dated for four years and fell in love. Since I was a northerner transplanted in the south, I thought it only appropriate that I act as a traditional southern boy and ask her father if I could have his daughter's hand in marriage. I asked her dad if we could talk, and we took a walk on his huge farm. Walking out of the house, I was extremely intimidated by her dad's stature, but I had to do this, and I really wanted to spend the rest of my life with his daughter. He and I talked about my intentions and what marriage meant to me, and he gave me his blessing to propose to his daughter.

We got married when I was 24, and set out on our journey together. Clarissa was accepted to a program to further her education and become a radiation therapist, and I was just beginning my career as a paramedic, so my mom graciously offered us a small place to live on their property until we could get on our feet. We both had long commutes for work and school, but we were happy and were ready to tackle the world.

We decided that we wanted to start our relationship out on the right path, and decided that we would go to church together as a family every Sunday that we were able. We began to pray together as well, and that strengthened and deepened our relationship immensely. Our faith became very important to us, and we grew closer because of it.

Chapter

9

When I graduated paramedic school I was only 20, and truly couldn't believe I had been given so much responsibility. My friends and co-workers would often joke that I could administer narcotics and defibrillate someone's heart, yet I wasn't old enough to have a beer after work.

I turned 21 about a month after graduating from the paramedic program, and began to search for a position to use my new training and skills. I applied to one of the busiest and fastest growing counties in Tennessee, and was offered a position. I accepted the position and was excited to face this new challenge. This county was large and had a mix of densely populated regions and some very rural areas as well. The county had numerous EMS stations, and the paramedic teams worked on a rotation schedule, so none of the teams would be in a busy location for more than a few shifts. We worked 24-hour shifts, then had 48-hours off. This seemed to work out well, and I was excited to get to know my new partner and co-workers and get to use my new skills. I still remember the feeling I had when asked what I did for a living, and I could say, "I'm a paramedic." I was so proud of myself and what I had accomplished in such a short amount of time.

Shortly after I began working and getting as comfortable as I could in my new role, I was advised that all paramedics in the county had to be designated as deputy coroners. While I wasn't comfortable with this new title, it was part of the territory, so I was sworn in and received my badge. I had went to school and signed up to save lives, and now I was given a badge to pronounce someone dead on the scene. Life as a paramedic in Tennessee was certainly different than I imagined when I lived in Maryland, but hopefully I wouldn't have to use this new role very often, or at all.

Working as a paramedic was very exciting and challenging, and you never knew what to expect. It was hard for me to comprehend life behind a desk; I much preferred life in the fast lane. I worked ten days a month, made great money, was never bored at work, had an amazing work partner, and had lots of free time to explore my hobbies… how could it get any better than this!

I loved the outdoors and spent as much time as I could on my days off outside playing. I bought a fishing boat, an ATV (All-Terrain Vehicle), had a pick-up truck, and would go hunting or fishing as often as I could. Any other activity that was outside was appealing, and I never turned down a challenge. I bought a black lab, because every outdoorsman needs a furry companion. I got Magnum as a puppy, and he grew to be a whopping 110 pounds. When I'd come home after working a 24-hour shift, Magnum would see my truck driving down the dirt road we lived on, and he'd get so excited. He'd race to the end of the driveway, and run beside me as I drove up to the house, his tail wagging and his tongue hanging out. If you asked me, I'd swear that he was smiling because he always seemed so happy to see me. He knew we'd be going on some new adventure, and I believe it was as exciting and enjoyable for him as it was for me. He loved to go fishing with me, and take rides in my truck. When taking drives, we'd often stop at a drive-thru burger joint for a snack, and on-lookers would laugh when they saw him gobble up burgers in one or two bites. Everyone loved Magnum, and he loved everyone. He truly was the perfect buddy for an outdoorsman.

Stressed: It Changed Everything

I was in my early twenties, and I was feeling young, energetic, full of life, and indestructible. I had a very strong core group of friends, and most of them also worked in EMS or firefighting. We all understood each other's jobs, and could relate; we were part of that family of emergency workers, and that instant bond is palpable.

Chapter

10

At the beginning of my career in my 20's, staying up for 24-hours didn't seem to be that big of a deal, and it seemed worth it because I could look forward to 48 hours off. However, as the years progressed, I started to notice small changes, and the long shifts began to take a toll on me. On my days off, I would now want to nap, and I'd dwell on the things I had seen at work. I often thought, people may call 911 once or twice in a lifetime, and I was the one responding to their life-changing emergency. I was expected to stay calm and in control during extremely chaotic situations, and people often think of paramedics as superheroes, because they truly do have the ability to save someone's life. Handling the scene of an emergency can be a delicate balance that can often take years to master. Family members and by-standers can be distressed and act out in ways that they normally wouldn't, and they can be patients that we have to treat as well. It is a stressful situation for everyone, and learning to rely on that inner peace can be tough for anyone, but we were expected to do it numerous times a day in all different situations.

My partner and I had a great relationship, both on and off the job. Since we were together 24 hours at a time, we became great friends and would often hang-out outside of work. He was an amazing paramedic, and we seemed to be able to read each other's minds while on calls, and had great trust in one another's abilities. On a typical shift, we'd respond to about five emergencies, and we'd often switch from being the primary caregiver to the assistant/driver, so neither of us would get overwhelmed.

One afternoon we were dispatched to respond to a shooting victim in an apartment complex just a few miles from the station, so we hustled to the ambulance, and got underway. My partner was driving, so I was the primary caregiver, and as we responded I began to prepare myself mentally for whatever scenario we were about to face. We had responded to many shootings over the years, and all of them were different: it could be an accidental shooting, a domestic situation, a suicide, or even a BB gun accident. As we pulled into the complex, I noticed a large group of people in the community swimming pool, and they seemed oblivious to whatever had just happened. We turned the corner to continue on towards the address, and I noticed something lying in the road ahead in the distance. There was no one around, and as we pulled closer, it became clear that it was a body. Could that possibly be the patient? Why isn't anyone around? This was eerie. We approached cautiously and noticed a large amount of blood coming from the patient's head. I immediately thought that the guy certainly must be dead, but when I bent down to do a primary assessment and check for signs of life, he was breathing and had a pulse! Not only that, this guy was in fact a teenager. Nothing escalates a situation more than when your patient is a kid. I yelled, "It's a kid, and he has a pulse!" My partner, who was on the radio with dispatch to advise them of our findings, immediately grabbed the stretcher, and we loaded the patient into the back of the unit. We jumped into the ambulance to begin resuscitation efforts, and within a few moments the scene was flooded with police trying to figure out what had happened. Meanwhile, we were in the back of the unit, starting IV's and attempting to ventilate this kid, trying to do whatever we could to help save his life. The hospital was only three minutes away, so my partner asked if I was okay, and he hopped into the driver's seat to whisk us away. While paramedics like to help people on the scene, some patients need extensive care that can only be given in hospitals by trained physicians and medical staff. When we arrived at the Emergency Department (ED), the resuscitation team was ready, and we handed off the patient to the hospital staff.

It isn't uncommon for paramedic teams to stick around emergency departments to assist in extensive resuscitation efforts, and it was an opportunity to learn from each other. However, when there is a kid involved, everyone seems to have the same focus: save this life! My partner and I stuck around to help in any way we could.

Further assessment of the patient revealed that he had sustained a single gunshot wound to the head, and even though he had a pulse and was breathing, the injuries he sustained were incompatible with life: he would not survive no matter what we did. It is usually difficult to find anything good in these situations, but this patient was a prime candidate for organ donation. The physician decided to approach the family regarding this, and the ED staff began to prepare the patient for transport to a hospital in Nashville if and when the family agreed. By now, the waiting room was abuzz with police officers and family members, questions were being asked and tears were flowing. When the family learned that death was certain, the wails and sobs echoed through the entire department, and it's always heart-wrenching to hear such things, no matter what position you are in. The family was obviously distraught, and were trying to grasp the reality that their loved one who was full of life just a few hours ago was now at the brink of death, and there was nothing anyone could do.

The family agreed to allow the patient to be an organ donor, the calls were made to Nashville, and the family was allowed a few minutes with their loved one. While time is of the essence in these situations, my partner and I loaded the kid into the back of the unit, and we began our 20-minute trek towards the hospital. I have transported many patients to other facilities who have required a higher level of care, but this was unique because we knew the patient was going to die very soon, and there was nothing we could do about it. I was sitting behind the patient's head with a resuscitation bag, providing artificial breaths, with a heart monitor beside me, beeping with every heart-beat. My only job was to provide breath for this kid, and just look at him and think. The rhythmic sound of the oxygen tank hissing, the steady beeping of the heart monitor, the siren blaring in waves, but none of those things were louder than my own thoughts. As I sat there, staring at him, and thinking, I became overwhelmed with the thought that I should pray for him in these last few minutes of his life. So I did; I prayed silently while I continued to monitor his heart and breathe for him. I noticed that his heartbeat was beginning to get slower and slower. I thought, "No kid, come on, just a few more minutes, don't die in this ambulance." I yelled up to my partner, "How much longer? He's starting to crash!" Just five more minutes, kid, come on, just five more minutes. We were racing through the streets of Nashville on our way to the hospital, and every minute his heart was beating less and less. My training had taught me what to do in these situations, but none of that mattered now, he was going to die, and we were just observers. I felt so helpless and wanted to do something, but nothing mattered, we just had to get him to the hospital, and fast. I continued to monitor him and breathe for him, and began to pray harder. His heartbeat became very erratic, and I knew the end was very near. I looked down at his face, and noticed clear fluid began to pool in the corner of his eyes and roll down his cheeks. Was he crying? Surely not. He is unconscious, but they seem to be tears. I've never seen this in all of my years in the medical field. His heart had stopped a few minutes before we arrived at the hospital. A great sadness washed over me. We pulled into the hospital, and instead of handing off a patient that was alive and full of hope, I was giving them a body for organ donation. We cleaned up the unit and made the trip back to the station in silence. Nothing needed to be said; we both had to process this and be ready for the next call as soon as we hit the station.

Stressed: It Changed Everything

Chapter

11

Dealing with stressful situations was part of the job as a paramedic, in fact, it was the norm. It is what we signed up for, and in the beginning we seemed to thrive in that environment. We lived from adrenaline rush to adrenaline rush.

My partner and I had just completed a rotation at one of the busier stations in the county, and it was time for a few shifts at another station. This station was in a rural area, and we usually had fewer calls, and we looked forward to a much needed break. However, we wouldn't have much of a break over these three shifts.

Stressed: It Changed Everything

We arrived at the station, completed our morning duties, then sat back to enjoy a little peace and quiet in the country. We were relaxing and talking, when we were dispatched to our first call of the shift, chest pains. You never know what to expect with these calls, it could be a minor thing like a pulled muscle, or a full cardiac arrest. We arrived on the scene, and the patient was in fact having a major heart attack. We treated the patient, and he was in critical condition as we transported him to the hospital. We went back in service, and not long after, we were dispatched to a cardiac arrest. Another critical patient transported to the hospital. Back in service. Yet again, dispatched to an unconscious patient. A stroke. Back to the hospital with another critical patient. We were exhausted and ready for the shift to be over. This wasn't a break at all, and I was ready for my two days off.

During my days off I often thought about the outcome of my patients, and would often have the intentions of stopping by to see how they were doing, but when you report for your next shift, it starts all over again, and there is little time, and sometimes it seems best to just let it go and move on.

We reported for our next shift. Hopefully, this will be better than the last, and we can rest a bit. This plan wasn't in the cards for us though. We were dispatched to our first call. A critical patient. Transport to the hospital. Back in service. Dispatched again to another critical patient. Back to the hospital. Back in service. Another call. Another patient that may die as a result of their illness. We pressed through the shift, hoping that this would be the end of the cycle; six critical patients over two shifts.

Our next shift at that station saw the same trend in this pattern. Three critical patients. We were exhausted. We had seen nine critical patients over the past three shifts, and every one of them we weren't sure of the outcome.

I often reflect back on those three shifts and those nine patients in a row whose lives were in the balance and could've gone either way. As the years went on, occasionally we would receive feedback on how a patient was doing, but I'd rarely ask or check on my own. I suppose I thought it was a defense mechanism, and a healthy way to deal with my job, but it didn't always work out that way. In all my years in EMS, that was the only time I transported nine patients in a row that were all serious and critical. Unfortunately, all these little stones were piling up and creating a mountain in my life.

Stressed: It Changed Everything

Chapter

12

Some emergencies are tougher to deal with than others. Some of the toughest patients for me were burn victims. As a medical provider, you can feel helpless, because no matter what you do, the patient is in severe pain. Medications don't always work, and treatment is tough because their skin may fall off at the slightest touch. On top of all this, the smell of burning flesh is unlike anything else, and seems to get stuck in your nose, and you smell it for days. In the long term, burn patients can often get much worse before they get better because of infections and swelling.

One fall afternoon, my partner and I responded to a burn victim in a salvage yard. As we approached the scene, we were given an update that the patient had sustained burns to more than 50% of his body. My partner and I discussed which roles we'd take with the patient, and I began my normal routine of preparing mentally for the worst possible scenario. We arrived on the scene, and we saw no evidence of anything burning. We drove up to the garage, and suddenly a guy appears from the building. He was slowly walking toward us with his arms out to his side; this was our patient. The skin on the top half of his body and arms was charred black and covered with blisters. As we got closer, we noticed that he also had patches of flesh that were hanging from him. We immediately ran to the patient to help him. I said, "Hang on buddy, and let us get the stretcher for you." As I said this, I lightly placed my hand on his arm to help him. He yelled in pain, and said, "Please don't touch me. I am hurting so bad." As I moved my hand away, I noticed that the skin on the area I had touched was now crumbling, and part of his flesh was still on my glove. We were faced with quite a dilemma; we had to touch this man in order to help him, and because he was so badly burned, there was no avoiding contact with his wounds.

We finally got him seated on the stretcher in the ambulance, and while starting IV's and placing him on oxygen, we began to talk with him about what happened, so we could get a clearer picture of the type of burns we were dealing with and how to treat them. He was welding a vehicle, and gasoline fumes caught fire and he was consumed with the flames. He received second and third degree burns to his entire abdomen, chest, arms, hands, and face. He was awake and coherent through all of our treatment, and was able to hold an intelligent conversation with us, even though you could see in his eyes that he was in severe pain. We continued to treat the patient and the burns, and give as much pain medication as we could, without much relief. We asked for assistance from the police department, and an officer drove our unit to the emergency room, while we both stayed in the back to provide treatment.

We arrived at the ED and the team treated him swiftly and aggressively, and they determined that he needed to be transported to the burn center. My partner and I were still at the hospital cleaning our unit, and dispatch called us to let us know that we'd be taking him to the burn center in Nashville, about 45 minutes away. I went back into the room, and found the patient in much better spirits than when we had dropped him off. His body was covered in bulky dressings that hid most of the burns, so you couldn't tell the severity of his injuries. His face was still exposed, and when he saw my partner and me he actually smiled and said, "Hi guys, they got my pain under control." We got him loaded into the back of the unit again, and headed to Nashville. We had a pleasant trip, and he was joking and seemed to be in a great mood, all things considered. I thought, "This guy will probably make it, with his great attitude and optimism." All through the trip we continued to talk, and I monitored his pain level; he was doing well. We arrived at the burn center, and the team began their assessment and treatment. I gave him a thumbs up and said goodbye as I backed out of the room. We cleaned up the unit and headed back to the station, not really speaking much. We were both really optimistic that his chances were pretty good.

My mind was consumed with him on my days off, and I thought that this patient was one I really needed to follow-up with and see how he was doing. I reported to work on my next shift and learned that he had died shortly after due to complications. I was not expecting this at all, and it hit me hard. This was just one more deposit of the reality of dealing with patients as an emergency provider. For weeks after that incident, anytime I smelled a fireplace or a brush burning, or even someone grilling food, it quickly brought back to my mind that really nice guy whose life I touched, and he never made it out of the hospital.

Chapter

13

At the beginning of my career, I'd come home from work and Clarissa and I would have breakfast together. We were newlyweds, and wanted to share every minute we could with each other. She'd ask me how work was, and I'd go over the day with her, and would often tell her all the details. This was not flattering talk to have while eating breakfast first thing in the morning, but we were in love, and just being with each other and sharing everything is what mattered. I'm sure she didn't care about all the gruesome details, but she let me ramble and get it out of my system.

However, as the years went by, I really started to become affected by the job. The change was happening gradually over the years, so I didn't recognize what was happening. I'd walk into the house after a shift, and Clarissa would ask, as she always did, "How was your night?" I'd just grunt, "It was not good." As she was getting ready for work, I'd jump into bed and stay there most of the day. I'd wake up late in the afternoon, still exhausted. On top of that, I felt miserable and had a horrible attitude towards everything. While I was at work, I had to perform at such a high level and maintain my composure and stay calm and collected in these horrible emergencies, and I seemed to use up all of my energy and have nothing left for my days off. Was this any way to live? I was going through the motions at home, and giving my job everything. On my days off I just wanted to relax and decompress, but as time progressed, I was finding it harder and harder to relax and enjoy anything. I would often lay around and feel lazy, but I continued to feel tired and miserable, no matter how much rest I had gotten.

I tried my best to hide this from everyone except the person who was most important to me, my wife. If we ever got together with friends or family, I'd put on my mask and pretend everything was fine. I'm so thankful that Clarissa put up with me during those years. There was an internal struggle inside of me, and it was manifesting in ways that were not healthy, and I was losing the strength to fight it anymore. I was physically and emotionally exhausted, and I truly didn't know how much more I could endure.

Stressed: It Changed Everything

Chapter

14

One morning I came home from work and went through my normal routine of putting my uniform in the washer and going into the bathroom to shower. Clarissa was getting ready for work and was in the shower already, so I let her know I was home and said hello. I turned to leave the bathroom and noticed a pregnancy test on the counter. I was stunned. I apprehensively turned it over, and it was positive; we were having a baby! We were both excited and nervous at the same time. Maybe this would be the change I needed, and maybe it would shake me back to reality.

Clarissa's pregnancy went well, and the time seemed to go by really fast. Of course, that's always easy for the father to say, I'm sure Clarissa was ready to get that baby out of her. I took some time off during the last few weeks of her pregnancy so we could prepare for our new baby. During those few weeks, I once again found myself trying to relax, but was still unable to rest. My mind wouldn't turn off and was constantly running, and I'd lay down, and would feel miserable.

A few weeks later, we had finished celebrating Christmas with our families and were driving home after all the festivities. With a last name like Clauss, you can imagine what the holidays are like for my family! On the way home, Clarissa told me that she was beginning to have contractions. We went home and called her physician, and we were told to head to the hospital. Clarissa was admitted, and we were getting her settled into bed, and her nurse appeared. A wave of relief washed over me because I had worked with this nurse many times while transporting infants to other hospitals, and I knew she was an excellent nurse. As the delivery approached, she came up to me and said, "Eric, do you want to deliver your baby? I have already spoken to Clarissa's doctor, and he knows all about your training, and he's fine with it." I thought, "No way! I could barely watch the childbirth training videos in EMT class; I'm certainly not going to deliver my own baby." I opened my mouth to say no, but another word came out, "Sure!"

The doctor and the nurse came into the room, and we all scrubbed together. I was so nervous, and the doctor was talking with me and giving me hints and tips and reassuring me, but I honestly don't remember a single word he said. Clarissa was finally ready to give birth, and the doctor delivered the baby's head, and then he let me take over, standing by my side, and coaching Clarissa. I delivered the rest of the baby, and it was the most surreal and amazing experience I've ever had. I stood there, holding my newborn child, just staring down, completely oblivious to the world. I was jolted back to reality by Clarissa's voice, "Eric, what is it? What is it?" I could barely find words, and said while choking back the tears, "It's a girl!" I often joke with my daughter now, who is a teenager as I write this, that I almost dropped her because she was so slippery.

What a wonderful experience and a beautiful surprise to have a daughter. I'm so thankful that we didn't find out if we were having a boy or girl, and it was a joyful celebration. Our families had gathered in the waiting room and were waiting for the news, and were trying to guess if it was a boy or a girl. I wasn't ready to tell anyone just yet; I just wanted to be by Clarissa's side with our new daughter. The joy of holding her in my arms and feeling like I was on top of the world. I was a very proud father, and it was sure to change my outlook on life.

Stressed: It Changed Everything

Chapter

15

I started back to work a few weeks after the birth of our daughter. I felt refreshed, and was excited to tackle the world. I had a new attitude and a new outlook on life, and was looking forward to getting back into the rhythm of things. However, those feelings changed when we responded to the first call of the day. My partner was driving, and as we merged onto the busy highway, we began picking up speed; I began to feel anxious and started sweating, and an uneasy feeling came over me. In the past, I had felt very comfortable with responding to emergencies, and driving fast with lights and sirens blaring even gave me a rush, but something had changed. While I was home with my wife and my new baby I started to reconnect to the real

Stressed: It Changed Everything

world, and I began to notice how working in the stressful environment of EMS had changed me.

After a few more shifts, I was back to feeling comfortable again. I did begin asking myself this question over and over though, "What am I going to do with my life?" I didn't have an answer, but I was beginning to think that it would be difficult for me to keep up the pace of working in EMS for much longer. Clarissa and I were beginning to talk about family, and how many children we wanted to have, and in what direction we wanted our family to grow. When I thought of the family scenario, it was difficult for me to envision EMS as part of that picture.

Chapter

16

Working in EMS, there are those calls that excite you, and you want to be a part of, and there are those calls that you dread and you pray will never happen. For many providers, a type of call that we dread more than anything are the incidents involving a child.

A few months had passed since the birth of my daughter, and I was falling back into the same pattern of working and feeling fatigued, but I pressed on. One afternoon our pagers went off, and we heard, "Respond to an infant not breathing." We raced to the ambulance and started on our way. I was going over in my mind all the protocols and procedures for whatever situation we were about to face. John and I had worked together for years, and we quickly discussed who would perform what duties. We had gone through so much together as partners that in many critical situations we didn't even need to speak, we just knew what each other was going to do and when; this was team-work at its finest. Nothing elicits a stronger sense of urgency than responding to an infant in distress, and we arrived on the scene within a few minutes. John ran into the house to get the baby while I set up the back of the unit for the resuscitation.

A few seconds later, John appeared with an unresponsive little girl in his arms. It was as if time stopped as John crawled into the back of the unit and placed the little girl on the stretcher. The baby exhibited no signs of life, was ashen gray in color, and her limbs were dangling as we began to do our quick primary survey and decide what course of action to take. We began our treatment: hooking the baby up to the heart monitor, establishing an airway, and looking for veins so we could start intravenous therapy (IV). Even while doing all these advanced techniques that can definitely save a life, I knew deep down that there was probably nothing we could do to save this infant's life. To add to the situation, when we removed the clothes to assess if there were injuries, we noticed that there were signs that she was neglected and wasn't properly cared for. Now not only were we stressed with trying to resuscitate a baby, we were angry and questioning how someone could do that to a helpless child.

We continued with CPR, but were unable to find a vein for an IV so we could administer medications. This isn't uncommon with infants, as their veins are tiny anyway, and when there is no heartbeat, they seem to hide. Fortunately, paramedics are trained in a procedure to help in these situations. An intraosseous infusion is a needle that is placed into the bone just below the knee and allows medications to be administered directly into the bone, and therefore the medications enter the central circulatory system. This procedure takes a tremendous amount of force and pressure to complete and isn't for the weak of heart to see or do. I was closest to the baby's legs, so I reached up into the cabinet to grab the appropriate size needle, and I prepped the site. I grabbed the leg just below the knee and began to bear down and screw the needle into the leg.

At that moment, I entered into a nightmare. Everything stopped. When I looked down at the baby, it was no longer a stranger, but my daughter. My daughter was gray and laying lifeless on the stretcher. John was performing CPR on my little girl, and I was jamming a needle into her leg. I was paralyzed and lost all touch with reality at that moment. My baby girl was my patient at that moment, and it was as real as the words you are reading on this page. I couldn't move; I couldn't do anything except stare at my precious child, laying helpless as we tried to bring her back to life.

I was jolted back to reality by my partner yelling, "Eric! Eric, are you alright?" I shook myself back to reality, told John I was okay, and continued on with placing the needle in the bone. We continued to work that code for what seemed to be an eternity, and I did my best to keep my composure. Throughout that entire call, I couldn't stop thinking about my little girl and what would I do if this happened to her.

We prepared for transport and arrived at the hospital ED, moments later the physician stopped the resuscitation, and the time of death was declared. I immediately left the room and went outside to the ambulance to clean up and try to get myself together. I leaned up against the side of the unit, out of site from anyone, and tried to process whatever happened to me back in the ambulance during the call. I thought, "What was that? Am I losing my mind? Did I have a hallucination? Am I going crazy?" I was afraid and confused, and had no explanation, but there was no way I was talking about this to anyone! John came out, and we cleaned the unit together and headed back to the station. I knew we could receive another call at any moment, and I tried to prepare mentally for whatever we were going to face next.

Stressed: It Changed Everything

Chapter

17

I came home from work and Clarissa asked, "How was your night?" I just gave my typical response, "It was not good. In fact, it was pretty bad." I left it at that. To me, not telling her anything about my bad shifts was a way of protecting her from what I saw at work, and I also didn't want to relive and rehash all these things in my own mind. As for the incident that happened the night before, I wasn't even sure what that was, and I certainly wasn't going to tell my wife that I had a vision that our little daughter was dead, and I was trying to resuscitate her.

As the months went on, I was constantly reminded of tragic events that I had responded to and often replayed them over and over in my mind. It got worse though; I began to imagine my family as the patients or victims in all those scenarios. The thoughts increased in frequency to the point of becoming an obsession; I felt I had to protect my family. I would always think the worst of every situation, to the point of paranoia. If my daughter and wife went to the store, and the phone would ring while they were out, I'd immediately think it was the police calling to ask me to come identify the bodies. If I heard an ambulance, I'd think they were in a wreck, and I needed to go find them. If my daughter was taking a nap, I'd go check on her, thinking I'd find her blue and lifeless in her crib. The reason I could replay these situations over and over in my mind with such detail was because it was my life and my job for years. I knew every part of those situations, because I had lived them out hundreds of times with real patients. I didn't tell Clarissa that I was obsessing, nor did I share the thoughts I was having. My behavior obviously began to affect my relationship with Clarissa. I never acted out aggressively towards my wife or my little girl, but the constant phone calls to check on them became the norm for me. I would wake up numerous times during the night and would go into my daughter's room to check on her. I was always restless, irritable, discontent, and exhausted. There were days when I didn't want to talk to or see anyone, and just lay on the couch and get lost in television.

I still thought all these irrational thoughts were normal, and I just passed it off as I was a typical first-time father who was worried about his wife and new baby. I truly thought I was in control, even though things were spinning wildly out of control.

Stressed: It Changed Everything

Chapter

18

Several times a year, the county would get a round of EMT and paramedic students going through their clinical rotations for school, and John and I would have an opportunity to be preceptors and show them how life was in the field. This is a fun and exciting experience, for both the students and the preceptors, and while you do not wish for bad things to happen during a shift, you did want the students to gain experience that would help them perform in critical situations. It's always better to learn while others are around to help, instead of being on your own and second-guessing every action you take.

John and I arrived for our shift one morning, and learned that we would have a student with us for the day. Peter was in paramedic school and was an exceptional student. He was about 6'5" and built like a wrestler, and was very friendly and outgoing. John and I were quite pleased. We had a guy who could help us lift, was smart, and was really friendly. We showed Peter the ropes of checking in for a shift, going over the unit, getting familiar with your equipment and preparing yourself before you were on a scene. We were having a great shift and responded to several calls throughout the day; none of them were extremely difficult, but they helped Peter relax and allowed him to get comfortable with the working environment.

As the evening approached, we heard another team from our station dispatched to a motor vehicle accident on the interstate with a possible car overturned. John and I thought we should probably get ready because if the scene was as bad as it seemed, we'd get dispatched shortly as well. The interstate that came through our county had a high volume of traffic, and the accidents were always serious. It didn't help matters that some drivers seemed to think of the highway as a racetrack and would drive fast and recklessly, endangering not only themselves, but everyone else on the road as well.

As we expected, we were dispatched to the scene, and were already prepared to respond. The first crew on the scene reported a single vehicle involved with multiple patients and at least one fatality. John was driving, and I was in the passenger seat, and Peter was in the back. We maneuvered through traffic, which was at a stand-still, and arrived on the scene to find at least a dozen emergency vehicles on the scene. There were fire trucks, rescue trucks, police vehicles, and now two ambulances. Based on the report from the first crew on the scene, we knew the scene would be chaotic, and I leaned back and told Peter to stay by my side, so he wouldn't get lost in the sea of people. Lights were flashing, and the scene was lit by the rescue trucks. Police were attempting to assess the scene and direct traffic. I opened the door and went to step out of the cab when I noticed a puddle of some liquid with something laying in it. On the scene of an accident, your eyes can play tricks on you with all the lights flashing in the night, creating strobe effects in an array of colors. Fortunately, I avoided the puddle when I stepped out of the unit, but quickly realized that the puddle was in fact blood, and the object in it appeared to be part of a brain. Peter stepped out of the unit, and I immediately placed my hand on his chest to stop him, and to tell him to watch where he stepped, while pointing to the ground. He looked down, then back at me and nodded that he understood.

We quickly noticed two teenage females that were crying hysterically as they sat on the side of the road. A few first-responders were trying to comfort them, but in the middle of all this chaos, comfort is hard to find. We approached the girls and assessed them rapidly; they had only minor injuries, but were extremely distraught and hysterical because their friend who had been driving was killed just minutes ago, and they were sitting on the ground watching this event unfold around them, in all its gory details. John took over treatment of the two girls while Peter and I approached the upside down vehicle to confirm the patient was dead, and to make sure that there wasn't anyone else in the vehicle.

The car was mangled, and the roof was crushed, and there was no way to access the vehicle from the passenger side. We walked around to the driver's side and noticed that the body was covered, but it didn't hide the massive amount of blood that was around the vehicle. I looked over to make sure Peter was okay, and then we continued. I uncovered the body that was still trapped in the vehicle, while taking a deep breath to prepare myself for whatever it was we were about to see. There was a girl, still upside down in the vehicle, and she was mangled and was missing half of her head. It appeared that as the vehicle rolled over during the crash, her head came through the side window, and it caused a partial decapitation. We later found out that she was only 16 and had only been driving for a few months. Since Peter was a student, I thought this was a great teaching opportunity to provide insight and go over the details and procedures that a paramedic must follow when dealing with fatal crashes. We then looked at the dead body and talked about the injuries that happened and the possible mechanics of the crash. We covered the body again and headed back to the unit. We still had two patients with minor injuries that had to be transported to the hospital.

I was walking back to the ambulance and noticed that I was not affected at all by the scene and the events that had just occurred. It was just another call on another shift. This is not a good sign. I was heading down a road towards a disaster, and I had no idea how severe it was going to be.

Stressed: It Changed Everything

Chapter

19

It was a long and cold winter, but spring had finally arrived. I usually enjoyed the change of seasons, because it meant I could busy myself on my days off with yard and garden work, and preparing the house with whatever chores needed to be done. Clarissa was a stay at home mom, and it was really nice to see her flourishing in this environment, and developing a mother/daughter bond that can't be explained.

I had arranged to take a few weeks off as the season changed, and I was really looking forward to this vacation. Not only did I usually enjoy all of the busy work that came with owning a home, I now had a daughter to spend time with, and I really needed a break from work.

Stressed: It Changed Everything

The time finally arrived, and I was excited; I really needed this. It started out great, and Clarissa and I were enjoying each other, and our daughter seemed to be the happiest little girl in the world. I was still unable to relax, and it was getting worse as the days progressed. I tried to hide it and force myself to be up and about, but that even made me more miserable inside. I'd get restless at night and couldn't sleep, and laying down caused anxiousness and irritability unlike anything I had experienced in the past. I also noticed that the thoughts I was having of my family being killed were coming more frequently and would often wake me in the middle of the night. I'd wake in the morning, with only having a few hours of sleep and would be exhausted, and the overwhelming graphic visualizations would start all over again. I'd wake and immediately jump out of bed, afraid that my wife and my little girl would be dead. I couldn't get rid of these thoughts; no matter what I did and they were getting worse. "I truly must be losing my mind," I thought. As I wondered what to do, the thoughts would start all over again, exploding in my mind. It got to the point where it was all I was thinking about, it was all-encompassing, and it consumed my world. They were so real and disturbing, I thought I was about to lose control and forget all sense of reality. I really thought I was going crazy.

I couldn't take much more; I was overwhelmingly exhausted, both mentally and physically, and began to think that the only way to end this was to take my own life. Losing control was not an option, and I thought if I shared these thoughts with anyone, I would be an outcast and treated differently. So the only escape was to end it all, and I even had a plan. I knew how to do it quick and painless, and even rehearsed it in my mind. It wasn't that I wanted to die, I just thought taking my own life would be better than any other alternative that was playing out in my mind.

One afternoon, Clarissa was in the kitchen preparing lunch. She had put our daughter in her baby seat on the table so she could watch her while she prepared the meal. It was a beautiful sunny day, so I went into the kitchen to see if Clarissa wanted any help. We just talked for a bit, looking out the window as she got things together. We had no plans for the day and were just enjoying each other as a family.

I went over to the table and picked up my little girl so I could hold her while we were talking. I walked back and stood behind Clarissa and looked out the window while rocking my baby in my arms. Suddenly, my mind drifted, and I was in a situation where I saw a large knife sliding into my daughter's stomach. I saw the blood escaping from her body as she lay lifeless in my arms. The blood was pouring down onto the hardwood floor, and my little girl was dying. I was holding my daughter as the life drained from her, and all I could do was watch. This nightmare seemed to last longer than any other scenario that had played out in my mind, and even worse, it was more real than anything I had ever experienced. I truly was in a different place and had lost all sense of reality. After a few moments, I shook myself back to reality. My mind was numb and overloaded with feelings of panic. I gently placed my little girl back into her seat and walked out of the room. I thought, "What was that? Why is this happening? Is this real or am I dreaming? Am I having hallucinations? I must be crazy, and I am losing my mind. This is bad, really bad."

I did my best to get through the day, but my thoughts kept drifting back to whatever it was that happened in the kitchen. I was confused and scared, and wondered if I was, in fact, going to lose control and commit one of these acts that were playing out in my mind over and over. This was the longest day of my life. I usually took pride in my ability to control chaotic situations, and did this daily at work, but I was being defeated by the situation in my mind, and I couldn't control it. I was sure I was not going to survive.

As bedtime approached, I was extremely agitated and anxious. Surely another restless night was ahead, and I couldn't face another night alone in a dark room with just my thoughts playing over and over again. More than once I thought that this would be the last night of my life. I tried to lay down, but every time I closed my eyes, my mind would replay that terrible episode that happened earlier that day. I was deathly afraid to go to sleep, because the fear that I'd wake and find my wife and little girl dead was all my mind could focus on. I was terrified that my family was going to die tonight. As I lay there, tossing and turning, I repeatedly rehearsed how I would take my own life if I woke and found them dead. No longer were only the thoughts a nightmare, my whole life had become a nightmare. My world had changed, and it was now dark and shades of gray, and it was getting darker with each passing minute.

I got out of bed and went into the living room to watch television; maybe watching something mindless would quiet the thoughts in my mind. I drifted off to sleep a few times, and just prayed for the sun to come up, so I could survive just one more day.

Morning approached, and I was relieved, but it was short-lived. The lack of sleep, and the thoughts racing through my head were wearing me out, but I couldn't rest. As the day went on, I wondered how much longer I could endure this battle in my mind. Another night passed, and I did manage to get a little sleep, but it wasn't much.

Chapter

20

The next day, Clarissa and I were going to her parent's farm to stay the night. Although I was exhausted, I was relieved to be out of my normal environment, and hopefully this would be a change for the better. As we drove for over an hour on pleasant country roads, I decided that it was time to talk to Clarissa about what was happening in my mind. I wasn't really sure how to approach the topic, and thought of different ways to tell her, but it needed to be done. I am a man of faith, and when I made the decision to tell Clarissa about what had been going on, I had a sense of peace. I wasn't sure what course of action we'd take, but I needed help, and I couldn't face it alone.

When we got to her parent's home, we had some time alone. Grandparents love to spend time with their new grandbabies, and they quickly whisked our daughter away to enjoy her. We went into the bedroom to unpack, and I thought, "It's now or never." We sat on the bed, and I told her that I needed to talk with her about something very serious. She sat next to me and looked at me with concern and love. Clarissa had no idea what was happening up to this point, and I was quite thankful for that. I searched for the words and how to even begin to tell the love of my life what has been happening. I began, and told her that I was having difficulty with getting some thoughts out of my head, thoughts of past emergencies I've responded to. I went on to explain that she and our daughter were taking the place of the traumatized victims in my mind. I tried to be honest and let her know how troubled I was, but keeping the details vague enough so as not to worry her any more than I had to. She quickly responded, "Eric, this is not normal. You need to get some help!" I can remember thinking, "You really have no idea how much help I need." She went on, "We need to call work and see if they can put you in contact with someone." I could tell from her face, and how she was squeezing my hand, that she was concerned for my safety and well-being.

Chapter

21

I called one of the administrators at my job and briefly explained what was happening, and they arranged for me to meet with a psychologist. It was really difficult for me to process that there was a problem I couldn't handle. I worked in EMS, and I was one of the super-heroes that others were calling to help them with traumatic emergencies in their lives, and now I was the one needing help, this was a very humbling experience.

As the day approached for my appointment, I went over in my mind how I would tell some stranger what was going on in my mind. I had rehearsed what I was going to say, and once again decided to leave out all the gory details because I was convinced no one would understand. If I told someone everything, surely I would be committed to a psychiatric hospital. I was truly afraid to open up to anyone about my thoughts; people would surely think I was crazy, and I was embarrassed.

The day finally came for my appointment. I drove to the office and sat in my car, looking around to make sure no one would see me going into a psychologist's office. I really didn't want to go see a therapist, but I needed help. As I reluctantly walked into the office, I was greeted by the receptionist and was handed a stack of forms to fill out. I filled out the paperwork, hoping that no one else would come in and see me. The doctor called my name, and I followed him into his office. As I walked in behind him, the giant sofa in the middle of the room seemed to be the focal point of his office, and he gestured for me to have a seat. I was ready for a little small talk and to exchange pleasantries, but he wasted no time, and shot right to the heart of the matter. He said, "Eric, can you tell me why you are here today?" I had very little time to react or to even process what was happening, and his assertiveness caught me off-guard. I responded, "I'm having a little problem with some thoughts about my family." He asked what kind of thoughts. I explained my job in EMS, my role as a paramedic, and explained a little more about the thoughts, but didn't elaborate on all the morbid details.

He sat back in his chair and just looked at me with eyes that seemed to pierce my soul. He finally spoke, and proceeded to tell me what had been happening in my life. He told me about my thoughts, and even included details that I had forgotten or pushed out of my mind. He knew all about me, and in just a few minutes had pinpointed my situation and was telling me what was happening. I just sat there and listened, stunned and amazed. After he had finished laying out everything that had been happening up to this point, I told him, "That is exactly what has been going on, but I never thought I could tell anyone or even find the right words to express my feelings." I felt as if a huge weight had been lifted off of my back, and I could breathe. I felt an instant sense of relief that someone knew what was going on, and seemed to understand completely. At that moment, sitting there on that giant sofa, it didn't matter to me if he was going to commit me or tell me I needed extensive therapy; someone finally knew my secret, seemed to understand, and it was a huge relief.

"Eric, you are going to be fine," he said. Those words seemed to echo in my head over and over. He explained that it was normal for me to feel these things with all I had experienced. He told me I was suffering from depression and Post Traumatic Stress Disorder (PTSD). I was surprised to hear that I was depressed, because I thought I was happy all the time, but reflecting back on the last few years, he was definitely right. As for the PTSD, I had never heard of anyone in EMS suffering from this at the time, and I didn't really know much about it.

He shared a story with me of a lady who was having thoughts of killing her granddaughter, and the thoughts were uncontrollable. He told me that this lady was one of the sweetest and kindest ladies you'd ever meet, and she'd never hurt anyone. She was, in fact, suffering from PTSD, and is doing great today. He went on to explain a little more about the thoughts I was having, and he said that these were called thought intrusions. I had never heard of the term so I asked if he could elaborate. He further explained that thought intrusions are unwelcome, involuntary thoughts, images, or unpleasant ideas that may become obsessions, are upsetting or distressing, and can be difficult to manage or eliminate. The thoughts may become paralyzing, anxiety-provoking, and persistent at inappropriate times. These types of situations are life-altering for everyone involved and it truly does take a toll on those who experience them. Years later it is not uncommon to have reminders and significant recall of past events.

He had just summed up the past few years of my life in one little session. He followed up, "Eric, you might want to consider another line of work at this point." This was no surprise to me, but EMS was all I knew. Furthermore, I have a family now, and my wife is a stay at home mom, I have a new home, and I am well established in my career and have been there for eleven years... what else am I going to do? He said, "Eric, I can't believe you are sitting here in my office. You are a remarkable young man who is always in control in any situation, and you can handle any type of emergency call at work; things must've gotten really bad for you to turn to others for help, and for you to be sitting here is extraordinary." I believe this super-hero mentality had gotten me in trouble; no one welcomed or even addressed problems, and the attitude was often to suck it up and move on if you can't deal with it. I didn't see this as the fault of any one person or any specific employers; it was just part of the profession.

He gave me a couple of options for treatment: medication or start a stress-relieving routine. He also shared that it may be helpful to write or talk about my experience with others to help them, and in turn help myself. All of this new information was overwhelming, and I was just beginning to accept and process what was happening in my life; I wasn't ready to share it with others. I opted to start a stress-relieving routine instead of medication, and we'd reevaluate this plan over time to make sure it was working. Getting rest was a big part of the healing process for me, something that I had found difficult to do in the past, because of the 24-hour shifts that are common in EMS.

As I was walking out of that office, I felt like a new man. A burden had been lifted from my back. I now understood what was happening, and I knew that it was something I could overcome, with time. I could breathe much easier, and I was going to be okay. The world seemed to be a brighter place again, and it was almost as if I needed sunglasses, because I saw my world in vivid, bright colors. It was a good day, and I knew God had a plan and would use this experience for good.

Chapter

22

It was a great relief to both Clarissa and me to know that I would be okay. It opened up a new set of difficult questions that had to be answered, but we both knew deep down the decisions that had to be made. We had to move forward, for my health, and for the stability of our relationship. We took a few days to let it all soak in, and to set out a plan: I'd get a part-time job and go back to school, and Clarissa would go back to work and be the primary source of income for us. This was a definite paradigm shift for us, but we were both confident of the decision that this was the best path for us.

We knew that I had to leave the EMS field, and I was fairly certain that I could find a job using my paramedic skills in some other capacity. Even though the transition was not going to be easy, I didn't think finding a job would be difficult.

I met with my supervisor a few days later to hand in my resignation and talk with him about my decision. I didn't think this would be an easy meeting, but it was just another step that had to be taken for my sanity. He made no qualms about giving me his opinion on my decision, "Eric, this is not a good idea. You have been here for eleven years, and you need to think about you and your family. You are well established here. You make great money. Please think about this for a while." I appreciated his concern for me, but I stood my ground and told him that it was the decision that Clarissa and I had come to. He asked me point blank, "Eric, why are you leaving?" I wish I would've had the courage to tell him the real reason, but it was all so new to me, and I was still trying to wrap my mind around the things that were unfolding in my life in rapid succession. At this point, I was still fearful of the repercussions of my diagnosis, and I truly didn't think anyone would understand. In fact, I was even having a hard time accepting it at times, but I knew the direction I had to move. Rather than be honest and face whatever consequences it held, I simply stated, "I understand your concern, but I want to go back to school, and it's just going to be too difficult to do both." Not that the answer was completely dishonest, I just withheld the reason I chose to go back to school. He was very disappointed, and it bothered me initially, but Clarissa and I were firm in our decision. As I shared my good-byes with my friends and co-workers, I wasn't sad, but rather excited about the change on the horizon. I had a strong desire to tell them what had happened to me and to warn them to be careful, but I never did; I just moved on. I'm sure many of my co-workers had thought I was making a mistake by leaving, but Clarissa and I were sure this was the right decision.

Stressed: It Changed Everything

Chapter

23

I enrolled in nursing school, knowing that it could build on the knowledge and skills I had acquired while being a paramedic. I was also hired to work in an emergency room as a paramedic in Nashville on weekends. My job schedule fit perfectly in with my school schedule, and while it left little down time to relax, I felt at peace with the goal I was pursuing.

There were a few prerequisites that I needed to complete before I could begin the nursing program, so I began classes during the summer. Clarissa was now working full-time, and I was watching my daughter during the day and taking classes at night. I was tired every day, but was getting the much needed rest every night in my own bed.

Stressed: It Changed Everything

The summer that I spent with my daughter was a time that I will cherish forever. She was a little girl and wanted to do all the things that little girls love to do: playing with her baby-dolls, dance to silly childish songs, chase bubbles, laugh, and nap. While I had to swallow my pride at first, because I was the man of the family; I loved those times with my little girl, and watching her enjoy every moment as a new experience. We enrolled in a few day-camps that summer, and I attended them right by her side. In one of the classes I was the only dad with the moms and their toddlers, but I treasure those moments, and we still laugh at some of those experiences today.

Chapter

24

Nursing school was more challenging than I had anticipated. While my paramedic training certainly did help with some aspects, the patient care philosophy was approached from a completely different angle. In EMS, our main mission was to quickly assess for injuries, make quick decisions and initiate life-saving treatment, all while rapidly preparing the patient for transport to a hospital. Spending more than an hour with a patient in EMS is rare. However, in nursing, we were taught the process of disease, how the human body operated and regulated itself and how we intervene when that process breaks down. We were also trained about long-term care and how to implement care-plans to improve and sustain life in the long term. In nursing, we were also trained to be part of a team, operating with physicians, technicians, and other professionals to treat the whole patient; this was so different than being on an ambulance and making all the decisions. This was a new concept for me and took some time to adjust.

I studied hard and gave it my best shot, trying to keep up and process all the new information. I thought I was doing well, and maybe going into the nursing program as a licensed paramedic made me a bit over-confident. The time was approaching for our first exam, and I studied day and night, you needed a 75% to pass the exam, and I received a 72%! I failed my first exam in nursing school. Well, that just let all the air out of my ego. I was extremely frustrated because I thought I had tried so hard. Looking back now, I'm thankful that I failed that first exam, it was the wake-up call I needed that nursing school was going to be challenging, and I needed to apply myself and prepare as never before.

One of my professors that first semester was Dr. Sherri Stevens. I went to her with my frustrations and ensured her that I was trying my best. Dr. Stevens encouraged me and helped me understand how nursing school was different from the paramedic training I had in the past. She became a mentor and an amazing friend throughout the program, and often provided tips and hints on how to succeed in school, and ultimately in my nursing career. Her willingness to always listen and her ability to provide encouraging words help sustain me through those years. I have tremendous respect for Dr. Stevens, and she is someone that I still hold in high regards today. We still keep in touch, and she has continued to be a mentor and provide those insightful and encouraging words that always seem to boost my confidence.

I felt much different approaching school as a non-traditional student. I was older and had life experience, a family, and was already successful in one career. The students in our class ranged from 18 to 50 and had come from all different backgrounds. We were a potpourri of different individuals who all had one goal: to succeed in nursing school. Some of us were more diligent than others, but we pushed on together. I was on a mission and had my eyes focused on the prize; I was not about to settle for anything less than obtaining my RN degree.

A few weeks into our first semester of nursing school, Dr. Stevens approached me and asked if I was interested in becoming class president. At first I didn't even entertain the idea; I was studying day and night, while trying to balance having a family and working as well, I didn't think I could possibly take on any more responsibility. On top of that, I was still adjusting to having PTSD and working on a plan to keep my life stable. I respectfully declined, and told Dr. Stevens that I didn't think I was the man for the job. In a very delicate way, she told me she could see tremendous leadership skills in me, and the class would benefit from this. I pondered on her comments, spoke with Clarissa, and decided to follow Dr. Stevens' advice and run for class president. After a fun campaign, I was elected as class president.

Dr. Stevens and I became very close during those years in nursing school. I told her about my experience as a paramedic and my brush with PTSD, and she encouraged me to do something with the story. At that time, and with everything else on my plate, it didn't feel right to move forward with it, but her words always stuck in my mind.

As graduation approached, I learned that the class president had to give the commencement address, and I was extremely nervous. I had taught smaller classes, but had never spoken in front of large groups, and there were going to be about 500 people at our graduation. Once again, Dr. Stevens was there to provide words of encouragement and told me to speak from the heart. It was a very emotional experience, and it was difficult to hold back the tears, but the speech was successful. I learned so much about leadership during those years in nursing school, and it helped form the person I am today. At the time, it seemed to drag on and on, but I pushed through, staying focused, and ultimately came out with my diploma and a smile on my face.

Stressed: It Changed Everything

Chapter

25

While in school, Clarissa and I decided to sell our home and move. We looked for a new house that would be closer to her job, my school, and our families, to lessen the burden for all of us. We found a nice little house and uprooted our family, and this was a wonderful decision.

I still had to commute for school, but it was shortened by our move, and I was very thankful for that. Often, while driving home from school, my mind would start to wander, and I'd start to get worried about what I was doing and I'd begin to second-guess my decision to leave my job and start school and uproot my family. I'd often pray during that drive. On one occasion a sense of peace washed over me, and at that point I knew that everything was going to be okay, and I was on the right path. That peace surpassed anything I had ever experienced before, and whenever I get anxious about anything now, I can close my eyes and still recall that feeling.

I also started to develop a passion for self-development, and during those commutes I'd often listen to books on tape and lectures by popular motivational speakers. Usually, no matter what the author's topic was, it always seemed to lead into how to develop your leadership potential. I took a great interest in leadership, and began to read as much as I could on the subject. One of the first programs I bought was *Personal Power II* by Tony Robbins. I took the program seriously and listened to all of the CD's over and over, and can still recall what Mr. Robbins said on the last CD, "Completing this program should not be the end, but the beginning of a life-long of learning." I still can hear those words echo in my mind, and I truly believe it's one of the reasons I still seek knowledge in everything I do. The interest grew, and I added new authors to my list of favorites as time went on: Dr. John Maxwell, Dr. Stephen Covey, Les Brown, Zig Ziglar, Dave Ramsey, Dr. Wayne Dyer, Joel Osteen, and the list could go on and on. They all seem to resonate positive change and to keep moving forward and to stay focused on the goal. They collectively have provided an amazing education, and I can easily go back for a refresher course by just popping in a CD. There's only one way to change the future, and that is to change something that you do every day. If you continue doing the same things every day, you will get the same results. I wanted different results in my life, and I changed some things, and I can tell you that it works.

Stressed: It Changed Everything

Chapter

26

Shortly after graduating nursing school, I was offered a job in the critical care unit at the hospital I was working. I gladly accepted, and began to get some experience as a registered nurse. Initially, it was challenging for my mind to shift from emergency medicine to long-term care, but I adjusted and began to find the groove and get comfortable in my new position.

Things began to progress very quickly, and just a few short months after working in that critical care unit, a friend called to ask if I'd be interested in a change. He told me that a children's hospital in Nashville was hiring and asked me to consider it. I was hesitant initially, but I applied after giving it considerable thought and discussing the opportunity with Clarissa.

About a month later, I found myself walking into a large academic medical center where I was now employed as an emergency room nurse. I had gotten so accustomed to change over the years that this was not really a stress factor in my life, and I took it all in stride.

My first day there was anything but typical, but thankfully my years in EMS had prepared me mentally for the challenge. Working in the ED is organized chaos. To the untrained eye, it may seem that the staff is running around in all directions tackling hundreds of issues and juggling dozens of tasks, but it is really a well-orchestrated and delicately conducted symphony of professionals all trained in specific tasks and handling them to the best of their ability. It truly is awe-inspiring to be part of a team that functions together as a perfect unit.

I reported for my shift and met the charge nurse and my nursing preceptor, and I expected my first day to be a casual day of introductions, but that wasn't in the cards. The charge nurse, Jenny, introduced me to Autumne, my preceptor, and away we went. Jenny had been working in the unit for some time and handled the stress of being charge nurse with ease and grace that was truly remarkable. Autumne was an incredible teacher and just rolled with the punches, taking everything as it came as if it was second nature to her. That day was a very busy day in the ED; we received seven critical pediatric patients from helicopters, along with several from EMS, and a few more that walked in. All of that on top of the normal cuts and coughs that seem to worry parents and have them come to the ED for treatment. I went from following Autumne around to managing my own patients before the shift was over. Jenny, Autumne, and I still laugh about that day. That experience was overwhelming, but I loved the environment and the stimulation.

Stressed: It Changed Everything

Chapter

27

After just a few short months of working in the ED, I was approached and asked if I'd consider becoming one of the charge nurses for the 12-hour night shift. I spoke with Clarissa and accepted the opportunity. Becoming a charge nurse was an amazing step for me, and it allowed me to put some of the lessons I had learned to use, and it tested my leadership skills. I made mistakes, but I learned from them and moved forward. The pediatric emergency department was an intense and demanding environment, but very rewarding. I further developed my patient care skills, as well as learning to juggle many tasks and responsibilities. I was also becoming an excellent communicator because with the new role came many opportunities to speak with patients and their families, as well as provide the team with direction, and advise management about daily operations.

I was no longer dealing with the thought intrusions or feelings of the past, but I was having some residual effects of having PTSD. I do try to take care of myself with exercise, good nutrition, and getting proper rest, as well as feeding my mind and my spirit; however, I feel I have lost some sensitivity and emotions in certain situations. I have been involved in many cases and have seen unbelievably traumatic situations that resulted in the death of a child, but felt very little emotionally from the events. I'm not saying that it didn't bother me, because it certainly did, but I didn't feel the way I used to. It was almost as if I were an observer watching the scenes unfold before me in a movie, rather than happening in real-life.

One evening I was at work in the ED and a young child was brought in, he was talking with us, but because of the severity of his medical condition, he suddenly died. The team did CPR, and we attempted resuscitation for over two hours, but were unsuccessful. I was sad because of what happened, and I thought about it for days, but it didn't affect me the way death used to. The interesting part of the story is that while my feelings and reactions to tragic events has diminished, I've become sensitive to how others react to stressful situations and am now able to help them deal with feelings they are having because I have walked in their shoes. Yes, I am deeply saddened and heart-struck when these events occur, but sometimes I have a numbness to stressful situations; I have however turned it into a positive and I open myself up to help others. It isn't that I don't care, because that is far from the truth. I feel like I've lost one of my senses as a side-effect of having PTSD, but my other senses have become stronger, and I am now able to help others as a result.

Stressed: It Changed Everything

Chapter

28

After just six short months of being in the role of charge nurse, my manager came to me with yet another opportunity. She offered me a position to help build a pediatric emergency care education program. This program was to establish relationships with EMS departments throughout the state, as well as other hospitals ED staff members, and offer training on pediatric emergencies. I was overwhelmed and excited about the opportunity, and began immediately. I started to develop and present training on topics of pediatric medicine, and I was fortunate enough to have a team of professionals to help me in any way I needed, and their assistance was remarkable.

As my first presentation approached, I was excited, yet nervous. Those butterflies that had become old friends were now back. The presentation was to take place about two hours away from the hospital, and I arrived about an hour early so I could check and recheck everything, and practice my presentation over and over. I'm sure if anyone saw me pacing and giving my presentation to the mirror they would've thought I'd lost my mind. My first topic was pediatric assessment, and I was as ready as I was going to be. There were about 50 pre-hospital and hospital providers in attendance; a large crowd for a first presentation, but it was sink-or-swim time. The presentation lasted about an hour, and while it was a tough crowd, I managed to get through it with favorable evaluations.

The speaking opportunities continued, and I was developing into an effective communicator. I was presenting every week on a variety of topics related to pediatric emergencies, and getting more comfortable in my new role with every step.

Things were progressing well, and I had an opportunity to present at another regional conference. There were numerous presenters scheduled on a wide array of topics and they were expecting a few hundred people. I was excited and prepared for weeks to ensure my presentation was polished and effective. When I arrived at the conference center that morning, the audience was energetic and eager to learn. My old friends, the butterflies, were back because the setting for this presentation was a bit more formal than I was used to. The first speaker had finished, and the host began my introduction. I was standing to the side of the stage, my hands sweating and trembling. There is nothing more humbling than standing by as you are introduced, with someone reading off a list of your accolades to an audience, building their expectations for what is about to come. He finished, and said my name, and I stepped onto the stage to applause. The lights blinded me, and the stage seemed the size of a football field, as I made my way to the podium. I turned to face the audience to thank them, and it seemed like 2000 people staring at me instead of 200, but the spotlight was on me, literally, and it was my time to shine. My nervousness subsided after a few minutes, and before I knew it, I was interacting with the audience and going through my presentation. The crowd seemed to love it, and I did too. After my hour-long presentation was over, I was buzzing with excitement, and felt as if I were walking on clouds. I finally sat at my table to watch the other presenters, and the gentleman next to me leaned over and congratulated me on a job well done. His name was John O'Leary, and while I hadn't ever met or heard of him, he was the next presenter to go on. His compliment gave me a boost of confidence, and I was settling in to listen and learn. John disappeared from the table as his presentation approached, and I was excited to hear what he had to say. He presented his story of being burned as a child, and not only surviving, but using the experience to give others the gift of hope and encourage them; you can overcome any challenge if you set your mind to it. His presentation was powerful and emotional, and it moved me. The conference ended, and was a huge success.

I continued speaking and lecturing several times a week to audiences of EMS, nursing, physicians, and other healthcare workers. Our team has grown, and our range of topics has increased, and we continue to reach out to our community to provide the best training we can on pediatric emergency medicine.

Several years later, I saw John at another conference. I spent some time with him, and I shared an idea that had been on my heart; not only could he be encouraging while speaking to large crowds, his one-on-one approach was just as effective. He was extremely encouraging and gave me great insight and advice to pursue my passion.

Chapter

29

Our team and several other departments from the hospital met for a two-day off-site retreat. It was a team building program, and one of our activities was to share something that had happened in our life that very few people knew. I was feeling a little more comfortable telling certain people about my brush with PTSD, but had never really shared it in a group environment. My time came to share, and I told them that I was a PTSD survivor and that I had a vision of presenting my experience to others, maybe even on a national level, in hopes that it could help others and open the eyes of everyone of a real threat that few talked about. I shared in great detail what my vision was, and a hush fell over the group.

Stressed: It Changed Everything

Everyone was extremely supportive and encouraged me to push on in this pursuit.

I had built several relationships with people that I felt comfortable enough to ask questions about the effects stress has had on them. I was overwhelmed with the information I was receiving, and learned that many had similar experiences, but never knew what it was. I had multiple conversations with people who had thought intrusions for years, but were afraid to tell anyone. Sharing my story one-on-one seemed to have a significant impact on their lives, so how much more would it help if I shared it with audiences. People that had shared their stories with me felt that they were not alone, and could finally share their feelings and open up with someone who understood, and at times I'd even encourage them to seek treatment.

I shared with Clarissa many of these interactions, and she was very supportive. The journey had begun. I began developing my presentation, and it certainly was a healing process. Some of the aspects were extremely painful to re-hash, but it was something I had to do if I wanted this to be successful. This topic was very personal, and it was unlike any other teaching I had done; I was going to be presenting something very personal and opening up my life to public examination, a part of me that few knew about. I shared with my manager that I was nearly complete, and she encouraged me to share the presentation with others.

It was great timing, because we were planning another regional conference out of town, and I was scheduled to be one of the speakers. There were to be four one-hour presentations, and I was scheduled to be the last speaker. I submitted my topic, and the brochures were printed; there was no backing out now. I was filled with uncertainty because this was unchartered water for me, and I had never presented such a personal experience to a large group. I practiced over and over, and each time I could barely get through without being filled with emotions and crying. I certainly can't do this in front of a group of about a hundred people; this is going to be a disaster. I continued to practice and have faith that this was what I was supposed to do.

The day finally came, and the audience had great energy as the other three presenters shared their information on pediatric emergency care. As my time approached, my nerves got the best of me. My time finally came, and I went onto the stage and shared the story of my co-worker telling me about his thoughts while in the ambulance bay. You could've heard a pin drop in that room after I finished that story and paused to gain my composure to go on. I became very emotional during a few points in the presentation and choked backed the tears, but I made it through.

After the presentation I was overwhelmed by the response, and many of those who attended approached me and shared how powerful my presentation was and how it helped them. I was so exhausted from being on that emotional roller coaster for the past hour, but I was encouraged that my story had helped so many. Phil, one of the coordinators who had helped put this conference together, shared how powerful my presentation had been and invited me to present it again at an upcoming trauma conference. There were going to be over 300 people attending, and I gladly accepted.

I prepared for the trauma conference, and the presentation was a huge success. A few weeks later, the conference planner contacted me and said that my presentation received one of the highest evaluations of any presentation in the nearly twenty years that they've been holding the annual conference. I was honored and humbled, and knew that my story was impacting other's lives.

Initially, I was extremely exhausted, and it was emotionally draining to give that presentation, but that has changed over time. I now feel energized when I share my story, and I have shared it with thousands across the country. My goal is to bring awareness to the subject of stress in the emergency care professions and educate providers on the steps they can take to stay healthy in this demanding field.

Stressed: It Changed Everything

Chapter

30

Clarissa and I occasionally talk about the experience, and she's completely supportive of my decision to teach and bring awareness to this subject. She has also been a part of the workshops and presentations I present, sharing her perspective of what it's like to have a spouse with PTSD. I have had a chance to share my story with thousands of people, and the feedback I have received has been truly overwhelming and positive. However, there is one part of the story missing, and that is looking at this through the eyes of my wife. I had a chance to speak with Clarissa about her side of the story, and encouraged her to not hold back and tell me how she really felt. I then tested the waters and took it one step further; I asked her if I could make an audio recording of her responses so I could share it during my presentations. It took some convincing, but after explaining that I thought it would really help others to hear her side of the story, she finally agreed. Up to this point, Clarissa and I had never really talked about the past experiences in great detail, and the answers she gave me were quite revealing and shocked me. Listening to her tell her side of the story was a tremendous blow to me. Sometimes we can get so self-absorbed that we forget when we are going through something traumatic, those most important in our lives are also going through something just as traumatic because of our actions. Although I knew that I had changed, I never knew how much it truly affected her until the interview. During presentations, whenever I play the audio of the interview with Clarissa, there is a silence that is palpable in the room. I usually follow up by asking, "How would you respond if the person you love more than anything said these things? Would you listen? Would you get defensive?" Often, we don't listen to the feedback from those closest to us. Maybe it's human nature to only hear things we want, and from our perspective; but if we can truly open our minds and our hearts, and ask questions that will help us grow, and listen attentively while trying to understand their point of view, we can grow even stronger.

I asked Clarissa, "Seeing the presentation for the first time, and thinking back on our experience seven years ago, what were your thoughts?" She said, while choking back tears, "Thinking back was an experience that is very easy to push out of my mind. After you go through it, you really don't want to go back and re-live it because it was a very bad time." I followed up, "After you saw the presentation, did you ever think I was going through that experience?" She said, "Towards the end, I never knew how severe it was. I didn't think it was as severe as it really was. I knew you needed a change because it affected us; you weren't happy at work, you weren't happy at home, you were always irritated and irritable... and you weren't even happy that we had a brand new baby." That answer tore me up and nearly destroyed me. Here I thought I was keeping everything inside and protecting those around me, but my wife could tell, and we just didn't talk about it. I ended with one last question, "How did I change during the years with this experience?" She added, "In the beginning of your career, it was exciting, and we would often talk about your night and your past calls, but over a period of time the conversation would become less and less. When I'd ask how your night was, you'd often just say it was good or not good. You did not go into details, and I did not ask. You are a very positive person, and you were able to stay that way for a long time, but as the years went by your attitude started to change, and you did not have the same positive attitude. I remember looking at a picture of you holding our daughter, and you were very pale, tired, and had no emotion. After looking at that picture, it hit me; this was a life changing experience for both of us, and I am so thankful for God's grace. We could look back and focus on what we have lost, but we choose to look forward and focus on the future. We are very excited that people's lives have been changed from this experience."

All of Clarissa's responses opened my eyes to look at things from another point of view, and I now try to keep my wife in the loop with how I'm doing, and in turn I ask how's she's doing and really listen. I encourage everyone to come up with a few questions to ask those closest to you, and really listen to their feedback. You can come up with your own list, and the questions may change over time to be relevant to your situation, but I encourage you to try. And most important, listen to the responses, really listen, it is extremely powerful and will give you information that you otherwise wouldn't have. The questions that seem to work well for us are as follows:

- Am I always stressed out?
- How is my attitude at home?
- Do I have a temper?
- Have I changed over the years?
- Do you think I am a happy person?

Chapter

31

Have you ever had one of those days when nothing good happens? You deal with challenge after challenge throughout the day, and quitting-time just can't come soon enough? You are finally leaving work, and you know that you are a bomb with a very short fuse, ready to go off at any moment. During your ride home you start gearing up for family-time, or other responsibilities that involve your family or close friends. You maintain your composure, and you tell yourself when you get home, you are not going to explode and take your frustrations out on your loved ones. As soon as you walk in the door, someone says one wrong little word or looks at you wrong and you turn into a three-headed monster. The next thing you know, you are squabbling over silly things that really don't matter. I am sure most of us have had at least one such occasion, if we are being honest. This type of behavior will cause significant challenges in any relationship and can be detrimental.

The good news is that there is an alternative. Having a "time-out" in our family is no longer a punishment, but an effective tool that my family uses to keep the peace. If you ever find yourself facing one of those days where you don't think you can handle one tiny thing more, you just tell your loved ones that you are taking a time-out. No questions asked, no pushing, no yelling. They respect you and let you go to your corner, or the library, or the garage, or the mall, or take a walk, or whatever little private sanctuary you have created to just find some peace and quiet and serenity right now in your life. After you've had time and feel better, you enter the real world and thank those around you who have respected your wishes. This little exercise has a two-fold benefit; you feel better, and your loved-ones know you've had a rough day and to be gentle with you... everyone wins.

Clarissa and I have implemented this in our family, and it works. We sat down when we were both in a good mood and talked about the rules and developed a plan for when we are extremely stressed or just need to escape for a bit and rejuvenate. When one of us, or one of our kids, has had one of those days, we simply come home and say, "I need a time-out." After rejuvenating, we simply re-appear and thank them for respecting our wishes. It's as simple as that. I'm a firm believer that every one of us, regardless of what field we are in, need to practice a "time-out" occasionally.

I usually take more than anyone else in the family, but one day Clarissa had an especially taxing day at work, and on top of that she had to work late. She pulled up the driveway, and the kids were excited to see her. Just one look and I could see that she was exhausted, and I knew she had one of those days. We talked for a few minutes, and she finally said those magic words, "I need about a 30 minute time-out." The kids and I left her alone, and she propped her feet up on the couch. Clarissa fell asleep for about three hours that evening. The kids wanted to wake her and ask her questions, but I protected her from the barrage, and told them, "Mom is resting." We all survived without mom for a few hours, and when Clarissa joined us, she felt so much better and thanked us for respecting her needs.

Stressed: It Changed Everything

Chapter

32

Over the past few years, I have had the privilege of working with many organizations and departments while presenting my PTSD story. I've collected data using an audience response system, and the information collected has been incredible. In these multimedia presentations, participants have a handheld device and will respond to questions anonymously, and the responses are immediately shown on the screen. Below is some of the data collected from over 300 nurses, physicians, EMS providers, firefighters, law enforcement officers, social workers, and other hospital workers.

- Over 50% of the participants had 10 years or more experience.
- Over 80% of the participants knew someone that left the profession because of severe stress.
- Over 65% of the participants believe they do not have the proper knowledge or resources to deal with severe stress at their current workplace.
- Over 65% of the participants are affected more by compounded stress versus situational stress.
- Over 65% of the participants feel they are not coping well with their current stress level.
- 99% of the participants believe that stress affects their home life.
- Over 60% of the participants have had thought intrusions, and over 50% of the participants were not aware of what they were before the presentation.
- Over 85% of the participants feel fatigued and tired even after getting adequate sleep.

- Over 65% of the participants have strongly considered leaving their current position because of stress.

- Over 65% of the participants are not satisfied with their work/life balance.

- Over 75% of the participants feel that their loved-ones do not understand how stressful their work is.

- Over 70% of the participants do not read or listen to audiobooks related to personal growth and development.

I've had multiple conversations with administrators from a variety of organizations and departments, and I have shared this data with them. Some were extremely surprised and were taken aback by the data that was captured, and for some it was frustrating because they were not even aware of the challenges that were being faced by their employees. I would always follow-up with, "Now you know, and can take action to assist your team with the resources they need." Knowledge is power if you choose to use it.

While obtaining my master's degree in nursing, my project was to examine the effects of stress in a healthcare organization. I learned that many hospitals and organizations have an employee assistance program to help employees that are affected by stress, but many of the employees are not aware of what it is or how to use this resource. There may be a brief explanation during orientation, but they may not be reminded of the program as their employment continues. I've come to believe that all employees should have an in-service every year to explain the resources that are available and how to access them. I've also come to the conclusion that having a department representative that understands the services available and can help employees get to the appropriate services needed. The reason I am so passionate about this issue is because there seems to be a negative connotation when the services may be mentioned, and I think this stems from a lack of knowledge to what the programs offer. As a project during my master's program, I partnered with a hospital employee assistance program to provide education on what services were available, and the feedback was very positive. There were actually a few participants that reached out to the program for help within days of being presented the information, and commented that they weren't even aware of how stressed they actually were. All providers, regardless of their professional level or position, need to know what action can be taken if they feel they are affected by stress, and need to know what resources are available to help maintain a healthy mind in this demanding environment.

Stressed: It Changed Everything

Chapter

33

What can you do to decrease stress in your life? I've shared a few things that I do, but there is an extensive list of things you can do to help deal with stress in your life. Keep in mind that these items are not exclusive, and there may be other healthy things you do to help you deal with stressful situations in your own life. I encourage you to come up with your own checklist to make sure you are doing okay, and have a list of activities that you can do in your own life to help you cope with the stress we all face every day.

- Prayer/Meditation. No matter what your personal beliefs are, or where you stand on spirituality, prayer and/or meditation can calm your mind. It is completely free, can be done almost anywhere with no special equipment, and is very simple to learn.

- Proper Rest. We all love sleep, but some of us don't get enough of it. Not only is sleep important for our mental well-being, but we are learning that without proper rest our physical body can suffer (high blood pressure, heart problems). Do your best to set aside 7 – 8 hours a night to get a good night's sleep; your body and mind will thank you.

- Proper Nutrition. It's so easy these days to eat on the run, but the food we often eat while doing that has very little nutritional value. I'm certainly not one to condemn fast food, because I like it at times too, but I try to eat healthy every chance I can. Try to eat healthy and keep a balanced diet; healthy food can be a well-spring of life.

- Time-Out. If you feel stressed and don't think you can face anything or anyone else, take a time-out and escape for a period of time. You'll feel better, and your loved-ones will thank you.

- Communicate with your loved-ones. Your loved-ones probably aren't mind-readers and have no idea how you are doing unless you tell them. Talk to them! Keep the lines of communication open. If you do this, it will alleviate many problems and obstacles in your lives.

- Proper Exercise. Going for a brisk walk, run, bicycle ride, or even attending an exercise class can help burn off lots of stress in your life. Not only do you work up a good sweat, it helps clear your mind for a while. Go to the gym or park and get in a good cardio workout a few times a week; your mind and body will thank you.

- What inspires and fuels you. Discover your hobbies, and learn to play a little. Whether it be knitting, fishing, cooking, writing, gardening, or whatever else you can dream of, take some time and explore the fun things in life again. Take some "me-time" consistently and enjoy yourself.

- Personal growth. There are countless podcasts, webcasts, books, audiobooks and videos by a wide-array of authors who spend their lives inspiring others to push on and become better. Find a few that speak to you and take some time each week to learn something that will truly benefit your life.

- Prioritize and learn to say no. List your priorities and learn to say no to things that are not important and do not line up with your values. Be purposeful with your time and save energy for your most important event of the day.

Chapter

34

In 2013, the American Psychiatric Association revised the PTSD diagnostic criteria in the fifth edition of its Diagnostic and Statistical Manual of Mental Disorders. I thought it would be helpful to list the diagnostic criteria, but keep in mind that only a trained mental health professional can accurately make a diagnosis of PTSD.

Diagnostic criteria for PTSD includes a history of exposure to a traumatic event that meets specific conditions and symptoms from each of four symptom clusters: intrusion, avoidance, negative alterations in thoughts and mood, and alterations in arousal and reactivity. The fifth criterion concerns duration of symptoms; the sixth assesses functioning; and, the seventh criterion clarifies symptoms as not attributable to a substance or co-occurring medical condition. Full diagnosis is not met until at least six months after the trauma, although onset of symptoms may occur immediately.

The first criterion deals with the stressor. One of the following criteria must be met. The person was exposed to: death, threatened death, actual or threatened serious injury, or actual or threatened sexual violence, as follows: direct exposure, witnessing the event, indirectly exposed to the event, repeated or extreme indirect exposure to aversive details of the events (usually in the course of professional duties).

The second criterion deals with intrusion symptoms. One of the following criteria must be met. The traumatic event is persistently re-experienced in the following ways: recurrent, involuntary, and intrusive memories, traumatic nightmares, dissociative reactions (such as flashbacks) which may occur on a continuum from brief episodes to complete loss of consciousness, intense or prolonged distress after exposure to traumatic reminders, marked physical reaction after exposure to trauma-related stimuli.

The third criterion deals with avoidance. One of the following criteria must be met. Persistent effortful avoidance of distressing trauma-related stimuli after the event: trauma-related thoughts or feelings, trauma-related external reminders (people, places, conversations, activities, objects, or situations).

The fourth criterion deals with negative alterations in thoughts and mood. Two of the following criteria must be met. Negative alterations in cognitions and mood that began or worsened after the traumatic event: inability to recall key features of the traumatic event, persistent (and often distorted) negative beliefs and expectations about oneself or the world, persistent distorted blame of self or others for causing the traumatic event or for resulting consequences, persistent negative trauma-related emotions, markedly diminished interest in significant activities, feeling alienated from others, persistent inability to experience positive emotions.

The fifth criterion deals with alterations in arousal and reactivity. Two of the following criteria must be met. Trauma-related alterations in arousal and reactivity that began or worsened after the traumatic event: irritable or aggressive behavior, self-destructive or reckless behavior, constantly feeling tense and on-guard, exaggerated startle response, problems in concentration, sleep disturbance.

The fifth criterion deals with duration. The persistence of symptoms of the previous categories must have occurred for more than one month.

The sixth criterion deals with functional significance. The disturbance causes clinically significant distress or impairment in social, occupational, or other important areas of functioning.

The seventh criterion deals with exclusion. The disturbance is not due to medication, substance use, or other illness.

In addition to meeting criteria for diagnosis, an individual experiences high levels of either of the following in reaction to trauma-related stimuli: depersonalization (experience of being an outside observer of or detached from oneself), derealization (experience of unreality, distance, or distortion).

American Psychiatric Association. (2013). Diagnostic and Statistical Manual of Mental Disorders (5th ed.). Arlington, VA: American Psychiatric Publishing.

Chapter

35

I know some people that read this book will relate to the story I told you about my journey, and may even feel that severe stress has affected every part of their life. Others may feel that they are not going through as bad an experience as I have, but you can still take away the main principles. I understand that uncertainty may cause fear and confusion when faced with this significant challenge. What I would say to each of you is to take action, and focus on getting healthy. The hardest part for me was to face the truth that I couldn't handle it on my own any longer. When I opened myself up to allow others to help me, my life turned around, and I began to see results. It was tough, but worth it. Every one of you is a blessing to many people, and I want to offer you encouraging words of hope. We, as a profession, are able to aid and help people in the most challenging situations, yet it is very difficult for us to admit that we need help. I know, I have been there. The fact is, we need to take action now and seek assistance to improve the quality of our lives.

If you are considering pursuing EMS or nursing as a profession, I am a huge supporter and believe that the field has much to offer. This book is not meant to discourage anyone from thinking about choosing those fields as a career because it has been my life and passion since I was a little boy, when I'd dream of riding on that fire truck. It is a wonderful way to serve the community, and make a good living in the process. What I have learned from this experience is that with a conscious effort to stay healthy in the field, it can prevent or decrease the likelihood of significant challenges regarding stress. My career path has led me to a teaching position, and I now have the opportunity to share what I have learned with many others in the profession, and I feel the healthiest I have ever felt. Knowledge is power only if we implement what we have learned. It is the responsibility of each and every one of us as professionals to become educated and make a mindful effort to stay healthy, so we can provide for our families, our profession, and the community that we serve.

I hope you reach out to others and focus on maintaining your own health so you can love every day. Remember, there is only one way to care for others, and that is to first care for yourself. God bless all of you, and I hope that our paths will cross someday.

Stressed: It Changed Everything